Betting on AMERICA

Betting
on
AMERICA

Why the U.S.
Can Be Stronger After
September 11

James W. Cortada
Edward Wakin

FINANCIAL TIMES
Prentice Hall

An Imprint of PEARSON EDUCATION
London • New York • San Francisco • Toronto • Sydney
Tokyo • Singapore • Honk Kong • Cape Town • Madrid •
Paris • Milan • Munich • Amsterdam

Library of Congress Cataloging-in-Publication Data

A catalog record for this book can be obtained from the Library of Congress

Editorial/Production supervision: *Nick Radhuber*
Acquisitions Editor: *Tim Moore*
Marketing Manager: *Bryan Gambrel*
Manufacturing Manager: *Maura Zaldivar*
Cover Design Director: *Jerry Votta*
Cover Design: *Anthony Gemmellaro*
Interior Design: *Gail Cocker-Bogusz*

© 2002 Financial Times Prentice Hall
A division of Pearson Education
Upper Saddle River, NJ 07458

Prentice Hall books are widely used by corporations and government agencies for training, marketing, and resale.

The publisher offers discounts on this book when ordered in bulk quantities. For more information, contact: Corporate Sales Department, Phone: 800-382-3419; Fax: 201-236-7141; E-mail: corpsales@prenhall.com; or write: Prentice Hall PTR, Corp. Sales Dept., One Lake Street, Upper Saddle River, NJ 07458.

Printed in the United States of America

10 9 8 7 6 5 4 3 2 1

ISBN 0-13-046078-8

Pearson Education LTD.
Pearson Education Australia PTY, Limited
Pearson Education Singapore, Pte. Ltd
Pearson Education North Asia Ltd
Pearson Education Canada, Ltd.
Pearson Educación de Mexico, S.A. de C.V.
Pearson Education—Japan
Pearson Education Malaysia, Pte. Ltd

CONTENTS

PREFACE

For a generation, 911 served a special purpose for Americans as the telephone number we call to report a fire, to get an ambulance, to report a crime in progress, to get help in an emergency. As all Americans can never forget, September 11, 2001 became the day 911 took on historic meaning, when thousands of people were killed in a series of terrorist-initiated events that were breathtaking in scope: destruction of both 110-story towers at the World Trade Center in New York, a portion of the Pentagon in Washington, D.C., and the crash of an airliner in Pennsylvania. Soon, the United States and more than 100 other nations quickly mobilized an international response to neutralize terrorism. 911 became 9-11 for the entire world.

Globalized terrorism dramatized the global trends and developments that were already changing our world. All Americans felt (and were) both involved and endangered, realizing that there are no sidelines in the global environment created by technology. The two oceans that once felt like America's gigantic security blankets were shredded as we came face to face with the reality of an *anyone, anytime, anywhere* world—for evil, as well as for good.

Suddenly shocked into uncertainty, we reacted by feeling that nothing is as it was before. The nation and its people felt present shock and future fear, wondering what would happen next, feeling that anything could. In perspective, history sends a more complicated message. While much changes when a historic event overwhelms us, it is time to look much further and deeper, and to examine the relentless pace of change in our time. We know from prior experience that major events accelerate certain trends, cut off others, and speed up and slow down society-wide developments. In the 9-11 aftermath, what emerges is both predictable and unpredictable (the unintended consequences we so often hear about). Nations are forced to initiate changes long overdue and neglected. New circumstances bring to the fore opportunities that were otherwise dormant. As individuals, we are challenged to learn, to understand, to grow, and to rediscover our responsibilities—as well as to grieve.

This book examines the 9-11 trauma for trends and consequences for us as individuals and as a nation, and at exploring ways to confront, cope, and leverage these changes. Beyond the 9-11 trauma, we have lives to lead, duties to fulfill, work to do. We propose that Americans respond with a forward-looking approach. To do that, we must move beyond the uncertainty created by events that shake our world. To do that requires all of us to understand the changes already underway in our post-millennium lives, analyze the costs and benefits we are paying, and identify ways in which opportunities and change intersect. In short, we agree with the view that America—and the world at large—is confronting a new normalcy, one underway for at least two decades, but which has become urgently obvious as a result of 9-11. This new normalcy is neither simple to explain nor easy to adjust to or possible to avoid. We all must deal with it.

We come to this task with the view that history provides lessons and reminders from the past on what we face. Nor is history the only teacher. Social scientists have their insights, business managements their methods and responses, governments their policies, and technology its built-in imperatives. Together, they provide a holistic view of the changes underway, suggest where our nation may be headed, and show how individuals and organizations can cope and eventually thrive. While 9-11 will haunt eyewitnesses and TV viewers for the rest of their lives, it does not stand alone in history's catalog of horrors. As one 20th-century example, Britons alive today have childhood memories of the aerial devastation visited upon London in the early months of World War II. In our own history, the British invaded Washington, D.C. and destroyed the White House. During almost the entire Civil War of 1861–1865, residents of the capital feared invasion and destruction.

Our underlying premise is that we Americans can cope with what we are facing, but it will take effort, adjustments, and a proactive approach toward changes across the board. Not only will we recover and go forward, we will find opportunities in a changed world by drawing on individual, group, national, and governmental resources and values. Understanding what is happening and identifying what can and needs to be done is part of the coping process. As one of the founders of what eventually became General Motors, Charles F. Kettering pointed out, "The world hates changes, yet it is the only thing that has brought progress."

Over the years, your authors have observed how change occurs in American society in facing social issues and business challenges. One of us is a professor at a major university, the other an executive at a major corporation. We have spent decades analyzing and explaining trends and how to leverage them, ranging from the social and the political to the managerial and economic. As we observed the reactions of Americans, the media, and government officials around the world in the weeks following 9-11, it became clear to us that perspective and presentation of a go-forward approach were called for. Our combined experience suggests that the important challenge is to look behind 9-11 to confront the ways in which today's events and trends fit into a large mosaic, then to identify what we can do as individuals and as a nation.

The analysis and recommendations in this book are the product of a collaboration aimed at sorting out the rush of events. We recognize that there are many other blueprints to consider and realize that others will put forth theirs. What matters is the need to respond and to contribute to the process of confronting the *new normalcy*. The aggregate of thoughts and actions are a sign of American's strength and a potential source of workable responses. In terms of the national will to prevail against its enemies, every call to Americans to renew their lives and to resolve to fight terror strengthens our resolve. Nothing could be more American.

As to the book's origins, what has happened is so critical and potentially far-reaching that we felt impelled to put aside other writing projects to develop and put forth a constructive, rational perspective as part of moving forward. Our publisher and editor, Tim Moore at Prentice Hall, turned to his medium—publishing—and enlisted us in this project, earning our gratitude for his editorial support and guidance. The opinions stated in this book are, of course, ours, as is responsibility for its deficiencies, not Fordham University, IBM, or Tim Moore and Prentice Hall. We also want to thank the production team at Prentice Hall that worked so efficiently to bring this book to you in timely fashion.

James W. Cortada

Edward Wakin

THE BUMPY ROAD TO A NEW NORMALCY

*Nothing gives one person so much advantage
over another as to remain cool and unruffled
under all circumstances.*

THOMAS JEFFERSON

I n both the best and worst of times, major changes can develop relatively unnoticed and unannounced. Then, suddenly, a shocking turn of events calls attention to changes that are well underway—the Boston Tea Party, Fort Sumter, a stock market crash, Pearl Harbor, assassinations, September 11, 2001. The world then seems to change suddenly when actually, changes were already taking hold. Despite the attention that dramatic events receive, they don't make changes. They call the country to attention. The more we have ignored signs and portents, the less prepared we are.

First comes shock, then a time of uncertainty. The nation seems to stand still, then it becomes aware of what's been happening and reacts—strongly.

On December 7, 1941, Americans heard shocking news, and those who were listening to the radio never forgot that day. The Japanese bombed American Navy and Army facilities at Pearl Harbor in Hawaii, at the time a U.S. territory. Radios across the nation spread the news as Americans tuned in at home, at work, at their neighbor's, in country stores, at the local barber shop. The next day, President Franklin Delano Roosevelt told the U.S. Congress that December 7 would be "a day that would live in infamy" and asked for a formal declaration of war against Japan.

Very soon, Americans realized that things had changed, as in previous wars. For many, personal memories were still there. The U.S. had entered World War I only 24 years earlier and the Spanish-American War 43 years before. Even some Civil War veterans were still alive. In a matter of months after Pearl Harbor, a new normalcy had taken shape. Within six months, there was rationing of raw materials, later of food and medical supplies. Young men and women by the millions were going off to war. The nation focused quickly on the task at hand: to defeat the Axis and restore peace. It was clear-cut, it was personal, it was all-out.

On September 11, 2001, many Americans saw the traumatic events of that morning live on television and had trouble absorbing what they watched, as a second plane crashed into the twin towers of the World Trade Center. A jarring call to arms punctuated the realization that something earthshaking had taken place. Americans confronted problems and threats that were real, but unthinkable before 9-11. As America's heartland felt the shock radiating out from New York, the reaction in Wisconsin was typical. Citizens steeled themselves for an uncertain future. In the state capital, Madison, barriers were quickly put up to block vehicles from approaching government buildings. Soon, postal workers were implementing security procedures to protect themselves from anthrax. Even an ordinary 34-cent letter could look menacing. The governor appointed an antiterrorism task force. Newspapers and TV stations reported the battering of the economy, the difficulty of hunting down the terrorists, and the threat of bioterrorism. America the secure felt vulnerable, from barbershop to local tavern, from Sunday worshipers to Saturday revelers.

On October 25, 2001, Vice President Dick Cheney announced that America had better get used to a "new normalcy," one marked by greater security checks within the nation, in a new kind of war in which the number of casualties within the U.S. could exceed those incurred on the battlefield. That same day, Congress finalized passage of legislation giving government officials vast new powers to monitor telephone and Internet dialogues and to arrest and hold suspected terrorists. One adjustment quickly followed another. Long lines at airport security points replaced quick boarding by frequent flyers arriving at the last minute. Border crossings in North America began to look like entrances to military bases. Working on the top floors of tall buildings suddenly seemed dangerous, rather than prestigious. Lower became better.

What made the new 9-11 normalcy different and unsettling was the lack of precision about enemies without uniforms out to get us. Is it the neighbor whose children play soccer with our children? The research scientist in the next aisle? The foreigner signing up for flight school? What are the names and serial numbers of the enemy we want to engage and defeat? Where are they, so we can take them on with our cutting-edge military technology? What is their tangled web of support? How reliable are our allies? As U.S. government officials kept repeating to the press and public about a situation so fuzzy, so frustrating, "We are going to have to feel our away along; this is a new circumstance."

Nonetheless, the lessons from history remain the same. While sudden events shock us, they do not occur in a vacuum. Pearl Harbor is an example. Beginning in the early 1930s, American officials and citizens who took the time to notice realized that the Japanese did not hesitate to use military force to expand their influence in the Pacific. Just by reading a mainstream newspaper, Americans would have known that, throughout the 1930s, the U.S. and Japan had significant differences over the supply of oil, which the

Americans had and the Japanese needed. It did not take inside information and exhaustive analysis to foresee a confrontation with Japan, as various government officials began to realize by early 1941.

In the 1970s and 1980s, portents in the Middle East were there to recognize as various Arab states supported terrorism and sponsored acts of terrorism against the U.S. military, against embassies, and against individual American citizens held as hostages. As so often happens in history, individual events point to dangers on the horizon. Behind the events, there are underlying changes—trends in the making that provide the context for a new normalcy.

In confronting what is happening, there is another lesson from history to remember. In every critical situation, some people suffer from new conditions while others benefit. Those who benefit do so both by accident and by design. Those who keep their bearings realize that we can leverage our resources to protect ourselves, to optimize our efforts, to lift our spirits, to deal with uncertainty. In our response, an optimistic approach is in sync with the American experience. During the darkest days of the Civil War following Fort Sumter, President Abraham Lincoln kept making speeches that said essentially, "This, too, shall pass." His celebrated second Inaugural Address and his speech at Gettysburg were grounded in the proposition that the dark events of the time would be overcome and that the nation would not only survive, but it would thrive.

The message was addressed to a country that would have to recover from a Civil War in which nearly 18 percent of all soldiers died in battle, half of them buried in unmarked graves. Towns and rural communities had lost dozens—even scores—of its native sons in military units which were often populated by soldiers from a single community. A disaster in one corner of a Civil War battlefield could plunge an entire community into grief for a generation. The entire South was ravaged, homes burned to the ground, businesses destroyed. It took decades to rebuild the South's economy.

As difficult as things were, ordinary citizens and public officials overcame them over time through continuous, forward-looking efforts. The circumstances after 9-11 have become our reality and our challenge, the result of trends that have become entrenched, though not fully recognized. The way forward is essentially a combination of caution, common sense, firm resolve, and the pursuit of new opportunities. This calls for an assessment of changes well underway before 9-11 and for a confrontation rooted in reality—the reality of technology as the great facilitator and enabler; globalization as an overpowering centripetal force; decentralization as a driving force in business, geopolitics, and terrorism; and empowerment of the powerless as active players in the balance of power. These are the realities of the new normalcy.

TECHNOLOGY: THE GREAT FACILITATOR

Among modern nations today, the United States stands out in leading the way with advanced technologies as never before in its history. In fact, if someone wanted to find a silver bullet in our society, it would be the total collection of technologies already available and in use, as well as the knowledge Americans have and are using to develop even more effective tools. Various groups of Americans continue to worry about the effects of one technology or another in harming the environment or in eliminating jobs. However, the fact remains that this nation's economy has prospered since the 1840s, thanks in important ways to a vast collection of technologies that it either invented (such as the telephone and the PC) or exploited at least as well as any other society.

As far back as the Civil War, the death toll fostered the American penchant for innovations after almost every family in the nation experienced a loss of relatives or friends. A determination to develop technologies that would minimize loss of life became an essential design point in U.S. military strategies for the next 14 decades. Unlike the British army in World War I and the Russian army in both World War I and II, which relied extensively on the deployment of massive numbers of soldiers to win battles, America relied more on technology to do the job. The American military and its political leaders always sought to minimize deaths. President Harry S. Truman argued that the reason he authorized use of atomic bombs in Japan was to save the lives of a million Allied soldiers. President George Bush and his generals designed the Gulf War campaign to minimize American casualties; indeed, less than 400 Americans died in that conflict. The campaign in Afghanistan was clearly designed to maximize enemy casualties while minimizing American losses. One reason why the American military specialized in, and did so well with, air warfare throughout the twentieth century was its collection of technologies. In addition to limiting American casualties, it proved an effective way to wage war.

The nation's inventory of technologies that can improve productivity, decentralize work, and enrich quality of life delivers enormous benefits. The national highway system makes it possible to distribute goods quickly across the nation. Almost every building and home has a telephone. Almost every home has a TV and a radio. The Internet is more widely used in this nation than anywhere else in the world, delivering information and services widely. An extensive list of technologies improves economic competitiveness, and personal security, and meets other needs of the nation. In confronting the new normalcy and terrorism, we need to increase our use of technology and to find more novel applications. Just as technology can provide weapons to attack us, it can provide defenses.

Anthrax in the fall of 2001 is an example. There was enormous concern about the safety of handling mail because anthrax was found in correspondence mailed to various people around the country. Postal workers died, politicians were tested to make sure they were not infected, and thousands of incidents occurred where citizens felt their mail was contaminated, causing police, fire, and other public officials to divert their attention from their normal duties. As public officials explored ways and means to decontaminate mail, at least a partial answer was at hand: Reduce the volume of physical mail by accelerating the use of e-mail.

In the financial marketplace, banks have tried for nearly a decade to persuade customers to bank online. Companies have offered to bill customers electronically. (Among themselves, businesses had already moved en masse to e-billing in the late 1990s.) With the growing availability of the Internet, one wonders how long it will be practical to publish and mail catalogs to our homes. First-class mail has been declining for over a decade, replaced by e-mail. One can reasonably expect that 9-11 and anthrax problems will speed up the shift of communications from paper to the Internet. Computer vendors and software manufacturers know how to do that and are already pushing their case. It is cheap, fast, and safer than moving tons of paper. While paper-based mail will probably not go away in our lifetime, we can expect a vast increase in the electronic movement of mail. The trend was already evident in the aftermath of 9-11, as bill paying via the Internet accelerated.

TERRORISM AND TECHNOLOGY

There is a dark side, nonetheless, to the silver bullet of technology. As we move toward greater dependence on the Internet to receive and send information, any threat to that information infrastructure poses a major threat to the nation's security and economic well-being. In the world of the new normalcy, we will have to find additional ways to protect that infrastructure. This is far more than the normal data security issues that corporations and government agencies deal with on a regular basis. This is all about network security, a much more difficult set of problems that range from protecting transmissions to securing the nation's supply of electricity (production and transmission). Due to ongoing innovations in the highly competitive telecommunications and computing industries in the United States and in other countries, the probability of dramatically improving the security of the Internet looks high, even though we may experience some cyberterrorism along the way.

Because of the decentralized nature of the Internet, there is no one giant computer that runs the network. This makes a lethal attack nearly impossible, although hackers have been mounting attacks for nearly two decades. The most they have been able to do is disrupt individual pieces of the network and spoil files on groups of PCs. Both corporations and key government agencies (FBI, CIA, and increasingly, the military) have been developing know-how to counter such attacks, competencies that will now be used more extensively than before.

Of course, the dark side of technology extends beyond issues of data security and the Internet. It also involves science and the reality that anyone wanting to harm a nation has access to technology and scientific knowledge to use in producing weapons of terrorism. Terrorists are empowered in very dramatic ways. Bioterrorism's terrible arsenal, as *Time* magazine has noted, can threaten nations with smallpox, the plague, botulism, and hemorrhagic fever (a family of viral diseases). Around the world, laboratories can produce and contain supplies of disease-carrying agents. Bioterrorism, as a threat, cannot be eliminated by simply washing our hands after opening mail. Air, food, and water are all vulnerable.

A serious problem centers on nuclear power plants and the availability of plutonium, which can be acquired from ex-Soviet Union scientists and engineers or already has been acquired by rogue groups around the world. The destruction of a nuclear power plant by use of a bomb or crashing a plane into such a facility could create enormous health problems across a wide swath of geography. Officials of the International Atomic Agency are concerned about terrorists who could create a "dirty bomb" by wrapping stolen radioactive materials used in medicine and industry around a conventional explosive such as dynamite. They could potentially use it to make a significant area of a city uninhabitable for many years.

The pervasive irony of technological progress, as represented by the Internet, is that the same function of decentralization sought by the U.S. defense establishment as a protection against attack also serves the enemies of the nation. Because the Internet is so diffused, if one part is knocked out, messages simply get routed along other paths, using different computers to get to their destination. The Internet's portability, decentralized access, and global availability empower terrorists who are out to use technology for their destructive purposes. For them, the greatest value of the Internet is not the opportunity to hack someone's system. It is the ability to communicate and coordinate activities around the world. They do not need to centralize their operations. They can be scattered in remote locations and use cell phones attached to a laptop to communicate over the Internet with coconspirators around the world. In fact, that is how terrorists in 2001 frequently communicated with each other.

In confronting the new normalcy, we face a primary fact of modern life that is represented by technology. As far as the overwhelming majority of Americans are concerned, those who denounce technology miss the point. Don't blame the machine. Blame those who misuse its powers. For Americans, technology is the great facilitator of their success as a country, nation, and way of life. They are committed to technology as they reach out to it for solutions to problems and never more than in confronting the changes and pursuing whatever opportunities that are part of the new normalcy.

THE RISE OF GLOBALIZATION

Business leaders, government officials, and academics have been bombarding Americans, Europeans, and East Asians for a decade with statements about the job creation and other benefits brought about by globalization. With good reason. During the past thirty years, three fundamental trends have led to the celebration of globalization.

First, the democracies that came out on the winning side of World War II embraced the notion of free trade as one of the most important building blocks of modern economies. The logic was that free trade would facilitate creation of a middle class in Third-World countries, while in advanced economies the export of goods and services would enrich companies and whole nations. Success has crowned the approach. Free trade is essentially the ruling mantra of the day, with a history going back several hundred years

before gaining momentum in the second half of the twenti-
eth century. The establishment and operation of the United
Nations, many rounds of economic trade agreements, and
most recently, the creation of the World Trade Organization
(WTO) provided institutional support for the movement.
Large regional trading blocks in Europe with the Common
Market and in the New World with the North American Free
Trade Agreement (NAFTA) are generally considered to be
successful milestones on the road to free trade.

Second, the vast improvements in telecommunications,
the processing and movement of data (thanks to computers), and more effective transportation systems (most notably, commercial air traffic) created an infrastructure that
reduced the limitations of distance. The telephone is widely
available in all societies and is effectively ubiquitous in
advanced economies, where phones exist in over 90 percent of all households and nearly 100 percent of all businesses. In some societies, cell phones are used by over 60
percent of the population. Satellites and the Internet have
made it possible for businesses to operate more globally
with integrated operating processes and in many markets
around the world in ways not possible in 1950, let alone in
1900. The result is that commercial activities are increasingly conducted with fewer borders, with cheap, fast communications and with more and more nations basking in
the sunshine of free trade. Never in the history of human-

kind have global trade and communication been so easy or so extensive.

The third trend involves the spread of two related concepts and sets of actions. The first has been the creation and expanded use of international agencies that transcend borders. The United Nations is the most obvious example, but there are important others, such as the Common Market and the International Monetary Fund, all creations in the second half of the twentieth century. These organizations made it possible to establish global standards of behavior, law, and economic practices. That is why, for example, a mass murderer can be arrested in Bosnia, tried before an international court in The Hague, then imprisoned in Holland. The second related part of the trend has been the slowly developing set of legal and moral benchmarks for behavior that are appearing across the world, mostly in advanced Western societies. For example, the global trend toward eliminating the death penalty is putting pressure on countries that still impose it, such as the United States and China. Another involves the less publicized movement toward implementing laws that protect property and personal possessions from seizure and clumsy legal bureaucratic behavior. This has been most in evidence in what were the Iron Curtain countries, in Latin America, and now in parts of Asia, although too slowly in sub-Saharan Africa and in what was the Soviet Union.

THE PROBLEMS OF GLOBALIZATION

As positive as these three trends are, globalization and the new normalcy present problems. Open borders make it easy for terrorists to move from country to country, as became evident when police organizations all over the world began tracking down individuals involved in 9-11. They were popping up all over Western Europe and across North America, the two most wide-open land masses in the industrialized world. As already noted, the excellent infrastructure for communications also makes it possible for terrorists to stay in close touch with each other. Communication and transportation, when coupled with the long-standing trend of making information increasingly available, accessible, and inexpensive, make it possible to learn what to blow up and how to do it, and to stay in touch with fellow conspirators.

Globalization, therefore, presents a problem for governments, particularly for liberal democracies. The problem is simple to state, difficult to resolve. Over the past 200 years, governments have been increasing the free flow of information and increasing the civil rights of their citizens and foreign nationals. Periods of totalitarian rule, such as in Nazi Germany, Franco's Spain, or Mussolini's Italy, were discredited exceptions to the broad pattern of liberalism. Even the Soviet Union, which fell apart because it could not compete economically or politically in ways that globalization called for, is in the process of participating in this new trend. The problem is, how do we retain and expand civil liberties and access to information in the face of terrorist threats that can be addressed more efficiently by restricting the free flow of information and curtailing civil liberties?

No country has been more tested on this issue than the United States, which clearly and unequivocally laid out its basic position in a series of documents in the late eighteenth century with the Declaration of Independence, the U.S. Constitution, and myriad state laws protecting freedom of religion. Over the course of the next two centuries, this nation expanded the availability of information, freedom of speech, and civil liberties, curtailing them only in times of war. During the American Civil War, for example, President Lincoln suspended the right of habeas corpus, locked up newspaper editors, and censored telegrams. In World War II, U.S. officials placed Japanese Americans in internment camps and censored all correspondence by its military forces in combat zones. During the Vietnam War, some protestors were thrown in jail for expressing their views, and in October 2001, Congress passed legislation increasing the authority of state and federal law enforcement agencies to conduct wiretaps and read e-mail. Every generation of Americans has been willing to curtail some of its personal freedoms for the duration of a national crisis, most notably in time of war. Afterward, they were persistent in regaining those constrained freedoms. A healthy sign.

What do we do in the current situation, where normalcy means living on a wartime footing for an extended period of time in a struggle against global terrorism in all its elusive dimensions? First, let us recognize that in no war in American or European history did anybody know how long it would last. Overwhelmingly, forecasts on duration have been wrong, underestimating the length of a conflict. According to European military experts, World War I was supposed to last two to three months. Earlier, American officials thought they could wrap up the Civil War in 90 days or so. Who would have predicted that the Vietnam War would last seven years? What a surprise it was that the Gulf War lasted only 100 days! Arab-Israeli wars are often seen as a continuum, marked by pauses that are interrupted by low-level fighting between Palestinians and Israelis.

Among industrial nations, Americans and Europeans now live in a time of persistent peril—the danger of minor and extensive military action, concerns about physical security at home, and threats to the welfare of the global economic infrastructure. How do we reach a balance between personal security and free movement? How do we leverage the benefits of free trade while restricting the movement of terrorists, dangerous materials, and their funds? These are not easy questions to answer, in part because the specific circumstances involved in formulating policies and practices shift. If the past has anything to teach us, it is that we will tolerate constraints to personal movement and access to information. We will also monitor the physical movement of people and goods, with increased cost to all economies and reduced flexibility of action. Watch then for products and services that become less attractive to sell and buy.

What became obvious in the wake of 9-11 were the unintended consequences for globalization. The *New York Times* on October 14, 2001 published a photograph of a bar in Tijuana, Mexico. It was empty. Prior to 9-11, that bar, along with many others in that community, would have been packed with tourists and Americans going south for the day to have a good time. But with the fear of traveling, the owner of that bar, well over a thousand miles away from New York and Washington, D.C. and in a different country, was in financial trouble. All over Latin America, currencies dropped in value within days of 9-11; sales of raw materials, such as copper and zinc, came almost to a halt; and around the world, airlines from the U.S. to China experienced 20 to 80 percent declines in sales. The economics minister of Argentina, Domingo Cavallo, summed up the impact on globalization: "What is approaching is a deceleration of the United States and European economies in the context of a war against terrorism." He was pointing out the perils of the interconnectedness brought about by globalization.

Negative, unintended consequences rippled rapidly through a globalized society. Within two weeks of 9-11, airlines, hotels, shipping lines, and restaurants around the world saw sharp, dramatic declines in business. Airlines began laying off tens of thousands of employees; hotels accustomed to 80 percent or more occupancy rates either closed whole floors or entire buildings. People around the world saw the Twin Towers blow up and reacted quickly and simultaneously to protect their economic assets and to improve their physical security. What is different from earlier decades is the speed with which positive and negative by-products of an event emerge.

For Americans, that means we will personally have to know more about international affairs, keep up with and be a part of activities of many other countries. We will have to learn foreign languages, more world history, and political science. We cannot leave it to diplomats or senior executives in our largest corporations. Americans as a whole must become more worldly as they make voting decisions, support various issues, take actions on behalf of their families and careers, and better understand the potential consequences of their actions. The day may come when some Americans will ask the kinds of questions globe-trotters and families living abroad have always asked—In what society should I raise my children? In which economy will my children and their children be best off during the 21st century? Americans rarely ask those kinds of questions, but their immigrant forebears did. That is how they made up their minds to come to America in the first place.

THE UPSIDE OF GLOBALIZATION

On the plus side, globalization delivers the many benefits of interconnection, starting with global infrastructures to deal with crises and foster cooperation that transcends national boundaries. These include telecommunications, international governmental and regulatory bodies, multinational corporations, and both profit and nonprofit organizations operating around the world. Add personal relationships among national leaders, nurtured by state visits and exchanges at every level of government, along with ongoing contacts involving business leaders, academics, consultants, and experts of all kinds.

Gone are the days when, as in the Cuban Missile Crisis of 1962, the White House had to scramble to find people living in Washington, D.C. who personally knew Fidel Castro and could advise the administration on possible Cuban moves. Today, American presidents know national leaders personally, exchanging visits that are supplemented by frequent telephone conversations. As necessary, they send personal emissaries to hot spots at a moment's notice. From the United Nations to the Red Cross, the world is tied together by organizations working full time on the world's problems and needs, their efforts facilitated by personal relations between individuals at many levels of government.

While some observers worried in the 1980s and 1990s that national governments would collapse in the face of the growing economic power of large corporations, nothing of the sort happened. In fact, the historic trend has been toward more national governments. Nearly 200 now exist, almost double the number after World War II. In many nations, decentralized governmental entities, such as in Italy and Spain, add to the mix of governance and spread connections around the world.

The results are striking. When President George Bush put together his coalition to go after Iraq in 1991, it took him several months to organize it; his son created a world-wide coalition in less than 30 days. One could argue that the issues were different, that the players were the product of a different generation and so forth but in the end, what sped up the process was a sense of global community. Of course, the glue that held it together, a war against terror-ism, was enormously appealing to nations that had experienced the horrors of such violence and those that feared it. But there was more to it. Nations have become conditioned to mobilizing their resources in joint efforts. They have been acquiring the habit of working together on global issues.

Free trade, international monetary policies, environmental protection initiatives, and now antiterrorism all have become global projects. The implications are enormous. For one thing, it suggests that Americans do not necessarily have to bear alone the full burden of dealing with thorny diplomatic and military issues in the decades to come. Other countries—not just the U.N.—can work on these issues by cooperating via international channels that already exist. We can envision a situation where national leaders might hesitate before launching an initiative that would offend the rest of the world.

As the interdependence of economic, monetary, and political conditions increases, already a major consequence of globalization, increasing numbers of nations will have reason to work together in protecting standards of health, economic well-being, and environmental conditions. Political scientists have long noted that the best way to create a democracy and keep it going is to ensure the creation and preservation of a thriving middle class. While the critics of world trade point out that Earth's resources are dominated by wealthy nations, they forget that, even in the poorest nations, standards of living are higher than in their past. Poverty in such countries is magnified in comparison with rich nations. The historic trend has been a slow rise in the standard of living of many parts of the world, particularly in that middle tier around the Earth that straddles the Equator for a thousand miles above and below it. Meanwhile, a disturbing imbalance troubles the waters as wealthier nations get richer faster than the poorest improve their economies. This creates tensions because all countries compete, and those that fall behind resent the prosperity of the wealthy nations. This goes a long way to explaining why anti-Americanism is more evident in poorer countries than in wealthier ones.

To be realistic, there are limits to the positive, facilitating features of globalization. The world is still a competitive arena. The distinguished historian, David S. Landes, in his book, *The Wealth and Poverty of Nations: Why Some Are So Rich and Some So Poor* (New York: W. W. Norton & Company, 1998), points out that the benefits of trade have always been unequal. The comparative advantages of nations never remain fixed but shift over time as those who respond to economic conditions tend to do better. According to Landes, in all societies, "some people find it easier and more agreeable to take than to make." He also points out that advanced economies can protect themselves, although not completely avoid the pain of doing so, by pursuing trade, exploiting innovations in technology, learning from others, creating new knowledge, and pursuing new markets for goods and services. He ends his lengthy, well-reasoned book with a simple statement that captures an essential feature of citizens living in industrialized nations: "Educated, eyes-open optimism pays; pessimism can only offer the empty consolation of being right." Globalization facilitates our ability to apply that perspective. Given the nature of capitalist societies and recent trends,

globalization can be leveraged in the years ahead to preserve and enhance the economic standards and cultural
values of more and more countries around the world.

EMPOWERMENT OF THE INDIVIDUAL

Soon after 9-11, a pilot told his passengers that, if anyone tried to take control of the plane, they should get up
and seize the hijacker. A few days later, a mentally unbalanced passenger on another flight actually broke into the
cockpit area. Passengers immediately rushed the man,
overpowered him, and regained control of the situation. It
was a close-up of Americans responding to the challenge of
the new normalcy, a sign of the sense of individual empowerment and of personal responsibility.

Prior to 9-11, air passengers had been told for years
that, if their plane was hijacked, they were to remain quiet
and passive so that nobody would be hurt. The strategy
worked, since hijackers usually just wanted a free ride to
some other country. But the rules of the game changed after
9-11, when hijackers crashed aircraft into buildings, giving
passengers the choice of either dying that way or trying to
foil the hijackers. It might still cost them their lives. Or save
them, as happened with the mentally unbalanced passenger. In the weeks that followed the pilot's suggestion that
passengers take charge of their situation, passengers all

over the United States commented to the press on how they would do the same thing. They felt empowered and responsible.

The incident symbolized what was happening. Americans were being asked to take charge of their circumstances in a nation whose culture always celebrated personal initiative. This authentic American trait was dramatized in the landings of Allied troops at Normandy in June 1944, when American soldiers found that the German defenses differed from what they had been trained to meet. Because they faced up to their objective—to get inland as fast as possible and overrun German defenses—they brooked no delay. Rather than call back to commanders in Britain or on ships for orders on what to do, they took things into their own hands. With so many officers killed or wounded on the first day within hours of landing, enlisted men made decisions about how to move forward and what actions to take without asking for permission. The results were stunning: They broke through German defenses, devised new tools to cut through the hedgerows blocking their advance, and improvised tactics. Privates and corporals took charge of groups of men that normally would be commanded by lieutenants and captains. And it worked. Officers of both Allied and Axis military units commented for years afterward about this unique characteristic of American soldiers: They didn't need permission to do what was necessary to get the job done.

This feature of American society grew out of the necessities of frontier life, where often homesteaders did not have the benefit of nearby army units to protect them or law enforcement officials to keep the peace or government agencies to handle community-wide problems. They were on their own. This attitude, nurtured when Americans went West to settle the frontier, is still around. Throughout American history, institutional support for taking the initiative ensured the existence of an empowered citizenry and reinforced this behavior. Constitutional rights, the protection of copyrights and patents, the free enterprise capitalist system, free speech, and entrepreneurship all contributed to this characteristic. To be sure, alternative pressures to regulate and dampen this trend also have emerged. Censorship during war and laws against specific business practices (such as monopoly behavior) have surged and waned over time. But a sense of empowerment persists.

In the new normalcy, we can look for a resurgence of empowerment and a sense of responsibility. In the wake of 9-11, public officials reverted to a long-standing American practice of reminding people that all citizens had to personally be part of the vigilance required to ensure security. People had to report problems and unusual behavior or circumstances, individuals had to seize control in a crisis, and everyone had to assume responsibility for handling their mail very carefully. From the president on down, public officials urged Americans not just to leave things to the government, rather to take personal responsibility for security in the new normalcy.

9-11 AND ARAB-AMERICAN RELATIONS

Just as technology and globalization were changing our world without alarming us and without demanding attention, so did Arab-American relations move through ups and downs, with only occasional headlines when blood was shed. The Cold War was America's international concern. The first (and sometimes only) thing America and its foreign correspondents wanted to know and to report was whether a Middle Eastern country was pro-Western or pro-Communist.

Lost in the process were the realities and the complexities of the Middle East—until terrorism that reached across sea and ocean demonstrated the power of technology and the impact of globalization. Suicidal terrorists personified the meaning of "Anyone-anywhere-anytime" by killing civilians, destroying towering symbols of economic power, and shattering illusions of invulnerability. As with all wars, the war against terror started on one dreadful day. But it was not the beginning of the edgy and complicated relationship between a Western democracy and a complex group of Arab countries traumatized by the arrival of a new nation in their midst that they did not want and could not get rid of.

Middle Eastern countries do not constitute a monolith. The have their own schisms, radical regimes, moderate societies, fundamentalists, Sunni and Shiite sects of Islam, modern nation states, and loose collections of tribal alliances set up as governments. This enormous diversity of cultures and countries means that anybody who wants to understand the region, do business there, or fight wars against terrorists or any other group has always found the region difficult to understand and deal with. That makes simplistic generalizations misleading.

The region as a whole is politically and militarily very unsettled, even violent, and seething with more issues than the Israeli-Palestinian confrontation. In the past 30 years alone, Muslim nations have fought more among themselves than with the West. After World War II, newly independent Syria was caught in a revolving door of political instability and repression. Lebanon was torn apart by an enduring civil war that broke out in 1975 and led to Syrian intervention. Iraq and Iran have had their bloody conflicts. Iraq invaded Kuwait. From time to time, assassinations have signaled changes in regimes. On top of underlying conflicts within Middle Eastern politics, repeated Arab-Israeli wars have broken out since the late 1940s, punctuating ongoing violence in contested areas claimed by both the Israelis and the Palestinians. Because of the persistent warfare in one part of the Middle East or another, a dangerous state of violence and extremism of one form or another persists as a constant feature of the region. Even stable Egypt has experienced terrorism, ranging from the 1981 assassination of Egyptian president Anwar al-Sadat by Muslim fundamentalists to attacks on tourists. South of Egypt, Sudan has for years had a vicious civil war that occasionally spills northward into Egypt.

In such a troubled context, focusing just on the Israeli-Palestinian confrontation blurs an overall picture of the Middle East. There are complications enough in that confrontation. Israel sees the end of the conflict in establishment of normal legal national borders and peace, much like liberal democracies do in other countries. The Palestinians claim territory that is occupied by Israel, while Muslims at large consider the existence of Israel an abomination because it intrudes upon their holy places. Neither side has been able to budge, despite enormous efforts on the part of the last 10 American presidents to bring peace to the region. The high-profile role of the U.S. government in pursuing a peaceful solution, as well as its commitment to Israel's survival and its substantial military and economic aid, has led many Arabs to see the United States as siding with an avowed enemy. Henry Kissinger, long experienced in negotiating in the region as the secretary of state in the Nixon administration, recently concluded that "the parties are not ready for a final settlement." He has recommended that low-level negotiations continue in an attempt to bring the parties slowly to some interim peace agreement, with the involvement of NATO countries.

Iraq, Iran, and Africa (of which a great portion is Muslim) present other problems for United States in the region. As the Gulf War of 1991 clearly demonstrated and the ongoing low-level military activities with Iraq remind us each day, Americans can easily get drawn into ongoing conflicts in the region. To argue that this will be the case until the region runs out of oil is to avoid the immediate uncertainties of political and military tensions in which Americans are perceived as intruders, as favoring Israel, even as being anti-Islamic.

A BREEDING GROUND FOR TERRORISTS

Fanatics who are ready to go to the extreme of suicide are not born but made by circumstances, reinforced by their surroundings, and shaped by their origins. The hostility mixed with a deranged sense of mission that turns them into terrorists has well-nurtured roots. What they set out to do raises serious questions for Americans. Why do Arab terrorists target the United States? Why do so many Arabs, more than dislike, hate America?

Let's begin with the recent roots of terror in the Middle East. Beginning in the late 1940s and leading up to the first Arab-Israeli War, guerrilla tactics have been employed on both sides, by Zionists and by Palestinians. The same set of tactics was also deployed in fighting civil wars, in toppling various Arab leaders, and even in conflicts between Arab countries. So there is a large body of know-how and experience in using the tools and techniques of terrorism—an entrenched practice in the region, as demonstrated by ongoing incidents involving Palestinians and Israelis.

Enter the United States as a target for terrorism. While strongly supporting Israel from its founding, the U.S. has never hidden its concern over the supply of oil and has formed alliances, landed troops in the region, and even fought one war to protect that supply. To many Arabs, the Americans behave much like the colonial powers that occupied almost the entire region in the nineteenth century. These have included Russia, Britain, France, Italy, Germany, and Turkey, with the British the most visible because of their control of Egypt, Iraq, and their lifeline to India, the Suez Canal. Great Britain and America have nearly always worked closely together, as in Afghanistan today. To an Arab, that suggests the Americans are like the British and the other colonial powers that have exploited the region.

An additional factor is the growth of militant Islamic political groups who merge political and religious perspectives. Beginning with the rise of Gamal Abdel-Nasser in the 1950s—after he overthrew the king of Egypt and several years later seized control of the Suez Canal from the British—pan-Arabism has developed into local religious and political nationalism. The ouster of the Shah in Iran and the erection of a conservative Islamic regime in that country in the 1970s continued the expansion of conservative religious governments in the region. Every country in the area today has what we in the West would call right-wing religious groupings. These groupings either run a country (as in Iran) or are so powerful that their demands cannot be ignored (as in Saudi Arabia). Militant groups train members in terrorist tactics and deploy them to further their local agendas. Repeatedly, that has involved targeting the United States.

Over the course of the last half-century, in response to Cold War politics, domestic political pressure to support Israel, and the need to protect oil supplies, the American government has sided with various political regimes that promised internal stability. That led the U.S. to support from time to time oppressive regimes that various Arab republics have opposed. Saudi Arabia is a good example, but so, too, was the Taliban when the Soviets were attempting to occupy Afghanistan. The result is widespread criticism of U.S. policies and less Arab condemnation of terrorist attacks than America expects. This helps to explain why the Arab states in general publicly criticized the terrorism against the U.S. in September 2001 but did not provide ground troops to help root out the terrorists. The most the U.S. could get were rights to fly through their air space and, in a few instances, the ability to use local air bases.

Meanwhile, over the years, the creeping violence directed toward the United States failed to arouse the American public to a crisis level. Shock and indignation, yes, but not sustained outrage and demands for retaliation. The episodes were limited to newspaper headlines and TV footage about an embassy here, a group of hostages there, Marines killed during the Reagan administration, a U.S. Navy ship attacked in Aden. Only once before Afghanistan did the U.S. reaction reach the level of direct military conflict at the level of war, and that was when a major supplier of oil to the West, Kuwait, was invaded. The thrust of U.S. efforts has been consistent: to reduce the level of terror and tension in the region while protecting the supply of oil.

The key point is that a pattern of anti-U.S. violence was not effectively quashed by the U.S. The declaration of war on terrorism finally changed that situation as America set out to impose a penalty that deters terrorism and to neutralize radical groups. But there's more to the equation. Until the Israeli-Palestinian problem is worked out, America will be branded as hostile to the Middle East and to the Islamic values cherished by its adherents. Ultimately, it will be the Palestinians and the Israelis who must make peace by succeeding where the U.S. has failed, despite its strenuous efforts.

The new normalcy calls for us to recognize that the Middle East will probably remain highly unstable for years to come. The area's governments need to sort out a large number of regional, historical, economic, even religious tensions, many brought on by themselves, others exacerbated by European colonialism and the rivalries of the past 10 decades. Arab governments are paying the price of failing to create stable middle classes by capitalizing on oil revenues and of not addressing the harsh realities of poverty and ages-long competition for limited supplies of food and water. Meanwhile, religion continues as a powerful incendiary force that inflames the atmosphere, threatens internal stability, and motivates terrorist actions. The situation calls for recognition of a clash of cultures, which hundreds of years ago would have been called a rivalry between Christians and Muslims, a view still widely held in the Middle East but which seems anachronistic to Western minds. As the area remains volatile, to the extent that we can extricate ourselves from the ups and downs of its conflicts, so much the better.

Overall, for Americans, the new normalcy calls for different ways of thinking about many issues at the global level and a return to bedrock values at the local level. Some of these have been suggested in this chapter; others will be explored in detail in the pages to come. It all begins with attitude and a way of thinking and feeling about current circumstances. George Washington, the commanding general of the rag-tag army that ultimately defeated the best equipped and managed army of its time, summed up the challenge that echoes today. On April 30, 1789, in his first Inaugural Address as the first U.S. president, he said, "The preservation of the sacred fire of liberty, and the destiny of the republican model of government, are...entrusted to the hands of the American people." For us as 21st-century Americans, the objectives are clear and unequivocal:

- To preserve national security
- To protect individuals from physical harm
- To preserve a national way of life
- To ensure the viability and prosperity of the economy
- To bring justice and peace to various parts of the world
- To heal the pains of national tragedy and personal loss

These objectives pose major challenges to nation and citizen alike. In the chapters ahead, we will deal with their implementation and suggest approaches for achieving them. The overarching strategy on a day-to-day basis was summed up by New York Mayor Rudolph Giuliani, who urged us to go back to work, go out to dinner, return to the normal routines of life. President George W. Bush echoed a similar theme. The widow of one of the passengers who struggled with hijackers over Pennsylvania, Lisa Beamer, put it simply, "It's time to get back to life."

2

FEELING OUR WAY*

*I wonder if I can trust you. But then,
uncertainty is part of life's fascination, is it not?*

DR. STEIN IN *THE REVENGE OF
FRANKENSTEIN*

I t is nighttime in a local coffeehouse. The counter man, Dan, is carrying on a casual conversation with one of the regulars. The door opens and in comes a well-dressed man carrying two shopping bags. He asks whether there's a payphone available, and when Dan offers the house phone, the visitor asks him in a soft, slightly accented voice to please call a taxi.

---

* This chapter was contributed by Scott Schaffer, Assistant Professor of Sociology at Millersville University of Pennsylvania. Along with interests in resistance, social change, and social philosophy, Scott is Managing Editor of *Journal of Mundane Behavior* (http://mundanebehavior.org), an online journal devoted to studying the peculiarities of everyday life.

After the cab is called, the visitor asks for a cup of coffee. When the taxi arrives just a few minutes later, the stranger pays for the coffee and leaves. Dan mutters something about getting a $2 tip on a $1.50 cup of coffee and goes back to his conversation.

It seems like a wholly unimportant event, usually worth only a passing comment before Dan goes back to wiping the counter and talking to the regulars who make a stop at the diner a part of their daily routines. They know what to expect. The visit is friendly, familiar, and predictable. It happens every day, normally nothing to think twice about.

However, details missing from this vignette change the entire picture. The diner is in a small Pennsylvania town, which is predominantly Anglo in its ethnic makeup. The counter man is not Anglo. He is a mix of Italian, North African, and countless other origins he does not even know. Often, he is mistaken for Puerto Rican, African American, Italian, or Middle Eastern. The well-dressed gentleman who was so generous to Dan looked to be of Arab descent. And the date was September 13, 2001—two days after the attacks on the World Trade Center and the Pentagon.

Filling in these details changes our interpretation of this encounter. The counter man had been talking about his theories on the 9-11 attacks when a well-dressed Arabic-looking man walks in. He hesitates for a moment, and upon seeing Dan, spits out a word of Arabic before switching into

English to ask for a pay phone. He then asks for a taxi to drive him to a nearby small town that would make a great place to lie low. He then asks for a cup of coffee, and a few minutes later when the cab comes, he quickly pays for the coffee, leaves a tip that is larger than the price of the coffee, and rushes out to the taxi. On the man's way out, Dan gives him a "once-over" look that says, "I will remember what you look like in case the police come looking for you." After the man leaves, Dan mentions the tip, then speculates, "What if...?"

This is but one of the many small ways in which everyday life changed after 9-11. Shocking images of planes crashing into the World Trade Center were only the beginning of the changes we have faced in the way we feel. From anxiety about the countless strangers around us on a daily basis to second thoughts about our usual traffic routes, to an increased sensitivity to our surroundings, it is clear that the at-home quality which characterizes what might be called "mundane behavior" took a serious hit. We lost blind faith in the mundane—those routine things we do on a daily basis or encounter without thinking twice.

To gain perspective on our post-9-11 reactions, we need to examine our feelings about the behavior, actions, and circumstances that qualify as mundane—the fact that they are predictable, that we can trust in them, and that we have a sense of security that enables us to do these actions or deal with these circumstances automatically. After examining these foundations of everyday life, we need to explore how things changed after 9-11 and the kinds of challenges we face and opportunities we have for living better in the 21st century. Looking at these challenges and opportunities is a critical part of learning to live in this new social and historical situation and of adjusting to what lies ahead.

FOUNDATIONS OF EVERYDAY LIFE

The term *taken for granted*, which often has a negative connotation, is not negative in itself. We *need* to have elements of our life that we can take for granted in order to make our way in the world. *Taken for granted*, if we look at its full meaning, is often positive and beneficial. Think of the countless little decisions and choices we make each day, the numerous actions we perform to get through 24 hours. Just to get ready for work, we need to choose to get out of bed when the alarm clock rings, choose to brush our teeth, choose to take a shower, decide whether to eat breakfast, to take the car or the bus to work. After making choices, we still have to act on them, usually in a particular, habitual way. We make the bed after we get up; brush the top left molars first, then move left to right and top to bottom; wash and condition our hair, then wash body parts from face to foot, eat pancakes rather than oatmeal or granola. So even before we actually "start" our day, we have made decisions and engaged in different tasks, a list that does not include getting dressed for work and all the decisions that the routine entails, depending on what lies ahead during the day.

We make all these decisions and engage in these actions mostly without thinking about them. We surely do not ponder their basic *raison d'être*—why we have to make them at a given time or why we have to make them at all. They are a basic part of our lives, *unmarked* because they are taken for granted and unexamined. They are invisible, hidden, unnoticed as we go on with our daily lives. We count on them as parts of our everyday existence until something goes wrong. Occasionally, we will slip up and forget an element in this daily path—forget our wallet, misplace our car keys, leave our briefcase behind, wonder whether we remembered to lock the front door. When we overlook an element in this rote list, things do not work as well as we are used to, and we feel "out of sorts." This is, in part, because these unmarked elements that can throw us so easily out of whack are not elements of our lives that we pay attention to. We pay more attention to office politics or celebrity scandals in the morning news than to our daily basics. We think of our lives as made up of more than the routines we must go through and feel that we "do not have a life" when our lives become too routine.

Yet, our routine activities and day-in, day-out decisions, our way of doing things and relating to others do not merely take up most of our time. In large measure, they define who we are and provide the glue that connects us to the rest of society. Cumulatively over time, they constitute our identity as others know us and as we become who we are. They are intrinsic to our sense of identity and a part of feeling good about our daily lives. Upset the mundane, with its sense of comfort, and we are upset as individuals. We become uneasy, candidates for panaceas of all kinds—in work, drink, drugs, exercise, medication, tranquilizers. Before searching for remedies, it makes sense to look at what we need—predictability, trust, and a sense of security—human necessities that terrorist attacks like those of 9-11 set out to destroy.

PREDICTABILITY

In order for everyday choices and actions to become a comfortable routine, we must be able to predict what will happen. We have to know—knowledge gained from experience—that if we do X, then Y and Z will happen. If we are going to work, then we must go through all the preparations to get ready and to leave prepared, both physically and psychologically. We can predict the everyday things we are going to do because we have made them routine, and they end up "routine" because they are predictable.

It is no different with other aspects of our daily lives. When we walk past someone on the street, we have different options: say hello and smile, drop our eyes and avoid any kind of contact, or cross the street in an effort to ensure our personal security. City dwellers enter what the philosopher/sociologist Georg Simmel called the *blasé response*: We acknowledge the person in some small way and move on, hardly recognizing or briefly acknowledging their existence, taking little or no notice of how they present themselves, regardless of how bizarre. We have a kind of performance routine available to us, in which we say our lines and move on to "the next scene" (work, shopping, a bar or restaurant, our next passing interaction). We know that the response of the "other" is going to parallel ours, and we move on to the next encounter. The entire situation is predictable because we have learned from social conditioning (experience) how things are supposed to happen.

This predictability is a necessary and reassuring component of our daily lives. We have to know what the weather is going to be like, when traffic will be heaviest and how long it takes to get somewhere, what lies ahead at work, what to do when interacting with other people in various situations. Social interaction depends on predictability in both directions, on how we act and how others interact with us. Laws, social norms, and customs, whether written or not, all drive predictability, which is why so much of our socialization as children is devoted to interactional routines—saying "please" and "thank you," "hello" and "goodbye" in appropriate ways.

We depend on these aspects of social life for managing the seemingly endless set of interactions we have with other people on a daily basis. When we feel things are unpredictable—for example, when we move across town or across the world—we do not feel a part of a place. We do not feel "at home," the desired feeling in our lives. Nothing brings this home like being a tourist or recognizing others as tourists. People who are "tourists" do not act quite correctly, drive, or conduct themselves according to local custom. They do not "fit in," and we are not automatically able to predict what they will do.

The ability to predict what others will do has a reciprocal impact. If we cannot predict what others will do, we are not sure what to do ourselves. The unpredictability also confronts the other person, who cannot predict what we are going to do. For the sake of avoiding unpredictability and ensuring the smooth flow of people's actions or interactions, societies develop set routines that strongly govern these actions and interactions, routines we learn by virtue of living somewhere and experiencing how things are done. These routines, these predictable ways of acting, are fundamental to the establishment of a culture and a society. Though they may differ from society to society, they are essential and help to make social life routine, making it possible for us to go through our day without having to think about every little action or interaction.

TRUST

The predictability of our social and daily lives requires and engenders a sense of trust in those around us and in our surroundings. That we can roughly predict how people are going to act toward and interact with us enables us to trust a given situation, freeing us from second-guessing the response or ourselves. We can, at least tacitly, trust that a stranger to whom we nod hello on the street will not turn on us, but rather that he or she will reciprocate our non-committal greeting. In other words, there is a kind of mutual and implicit trust between people, even strangers, that each will act in accordance with the expectations of our culture and with the other's expectations.

At the same time, the predictability of daily and social life also requires that we can rely on ourselves and our personal infrastructure to function as expected and needed—from our bodies to our cars, from the home heating system to the telephone, from the electricity to the running water, from police and fire services to emergency ambulance services. We expect the family car to start because we trust its manufacturer, we trust in our keeping up with the maintenance schedule, and we trust the mechanics who have worked on it. When we cross the street, we trust that drivers will stop for red lights and turn in the direction of their signals. Whatever we do during the day, we take it for granted that others will follow the "rules of the road."

We take everyday things for granted in this chain of dependence that makes daily life possible, trusting all the public and private services, all the people staffing them, and all the people that we run up against: pedestrians, shoppers, drivers, restaurant workers, and servers. This trust is an essential part of managing our daily lives.

SECURITY—FEELING AT HOME

On reflection, the mutually reinforcing combination of predictability and trust serves as the fabric of social life. The acts that we perform, the choices we make, the interactions we have, and all the other stuff of mundane life rely on our ability to predict what others can and will do. This, in turn, governs our response based on our ability to trust others by knowing how they will act and how things will function.

Taken together as the "social contract"—the implicit contract between people that they will follow the rules—predictability and trust give us a third fundamental of everyday life: a sense of security. While security comes to mind as something that is explicitly pursued—buying a home alarm or a car theft-prevention device—it is more fundamental and more organic. If we close our eyes and think of the place where we feel most safe, it is most likely our home. That sense of being *at home* is crucial to the normal functioning of our ordinary lives.

Being at home really means being a part of something larger than us—a family, a community, a city—and not having to think about or intentionally act to bring about that feeling. The Norman Rockwell version of "home"—part of what has been called the "nostalgia trap" of American society—is supposed to happen naturally, not require conscious effort. It happens that way in sitcoms, in stories parents tell their children about "how things used to be" when they were young. "At-homeness" is just there, and we need it in order to glide smoothly and effortlessly through the many actions we embark on every day, at home, at work, in school and stores, on local streets and national highways, at the movies, and in front of the TV. Even when we are away from home, whether on vacation or on business, we tend to stick to routines we develop at home.

The basics of everyday life discussed here—trust, predictability, and security—enable us to feel confident that things will operate as they are supposed to while we also refer to larger perspectives and mindsets for a sense of at-homeness. These range from the proverbial "God, home, and country" to faith in a particular religion. Knowing that these frameworks continue to hold true allows us to predict how things work, to trust in their operation, and to feel at home in the world. This sense of at-homeness is crucially needed so that we can live extraordinary lives, adding meaning to everydayness.

HOW THINGS CHANGED

Normally, this kind of discussion is relegated to university courses in sociology or articles in scholarly journals. But that was before 9-11. The all-inclusive war on terrorism has brought the issue out of the theoretical realm and into the practical. The effects appear in our daily lives. The real targets are us—or rather, our sense of the everydayness of the world around us—as we go about our daily lives, begin yet another workday, take the train, make a plane reservation, go to the office. The attacks of 9-11 made us all vulnerable, struck at the fabric of everyday American life, left us feeling violated, outraged, victimized, and ultimately fearful and uncertain about the future.

Our trust in "Fortress America" has been shaken. In the decades since the end of World War II, if not since the end of the Soviet nuclear threat and the Cold War in 1991, Americans viewed their country as basically impregnable to outside attack, unlike beleaguered nations all over the world. Of course, this was not entirely true. There have been terrorist attacks. The World Trade Center bombing in

1993 and the bombing of the Oklahoma City federal building in 1994 certainly were attacks *in* America, but they were not explicitly attacks *on* America, on what America stands for and on what America has done in the world. September 11 was. The attacks on the most obvious signs of American power—economic power in the form of the World Trade Center and military power in the form of the Pentagon—exposed Fortress America as vulnerable. We could no longer take it for granted as impregnable. We *could* be violated. If 9-11 could happen, what else could happen?

As security becomes a national preoccupation, the issue dominates reporting, public discussion, and commentary in the media, which then intensifies public attention and escalates individual concerns. Just as events during the Cold War were typically examined as pro- or anti-Communist, so after 9-11 any bombings, air crashes, or possible signs of terrorism are examined in terms of "terrorist conspiracies." Anxiety is magnified by ballyhooed actions to strengthen security, by any signs of security breakdowns, and by the entire process of building up "homeland security." Suddenly, Americans are confronting changes in everyday life, as reinforced by government warnings of terrorist threats and dramatized by highly visible security in public places. Legislation made possible the surveillance of individuals perceived as a threat to "national security," and military tribunals provided a forum where national security could be protected via the secrecy of trials. The United States became security-minded, with its citizens expected to do their part.

As individuals and as communities, we felt as though everything in our lives that had been unmarked before September 11 was now marked, up for questioning, review, and possibly suspicion after September 11. Everything predictable, everything that made us feel at home in our daily lives as citizens of obstensibly the most powerful and secure nation in the world, was no longer predictable, no longer matter of fact. As a country, we had to rethink business as usual, pay attention to security, and figure out the difference between real and imagined danger. College students in class began sitting close to the exits; people began looking up apprehensively at the sky when they heard a plane; and, after the anthrax letter attacks, even that most mundane of daily items, the mail, landed at our front door with the menacing sound of a threat.

The change highlights the difference between feeling at home and feeling secure. The latter is a tactical state of mind—being on guard, maintaining awareness, and anticipating the breakdown of things around us. It signifies a fear of things outside our control. The former carries with it a sense of happiness or contentedness, where we feel safe, not because we are hunkered down against any potential threat but because we are cared for and loved by others and feel connected to them. After 9-11, the feeling of at-home-ness gave way to the pursuit of security which, on reflection, had been going on for decades. Master-planned and gated communities and apartment complexes were built in response to the 1960s "white flight" following inner-city riots. They provide easily masked security measures such as roadway layouts that get outsiders lost and front doors that never face the street. In shifting from a rehabilitation model to a "quarantine" model, the criminal justice and mental health systems warehouse criminals and mentally disabled people far away from "society" for as long as possible. Security guards, video surveillance, and Internet-based surveillance protocols such as Echelon have become commonplace. In sum, Americans have felt for years that the world is threatening. When we trade making the world a place to be at home for the security of a bunker, the world "falls apart" even more.

A bunker mentality and quest for security pervasively affect how we act in public. We watch out for people who might be a "threat," whether a "city cat" in a small town or someone we have been told might be a threat. We cover our PIN numbers at bank machines and pay phones, guard our credit card numbers by shredding receipts and statements, and shop online only with companies that have secure servers and explicit security policies. We have been on a quest for security for years now; September 11 has accelerated that quest.

The war on terrorism and repeated alerts keep the issue of security in the foreground of our consciousness through a continuous barrage by newspaper, magazine, radio, and TV, thereby reinforcing a sense of insecurity. Creation of the cabinet-level Office of Homeland Security established the pursuit of security as a federal priority and reinforced the feeling that we cannot take security for granted. Uneasiness is an inevitable by-product. If the combined resources of the FBI, the CIA, the National Security Agency, the Defense Intelligence Agency, and the intelligence agencies of allied countries could not warn us of 9-11, it is natural to worry about predicting future attacks.

Finding it difficult to assuage the sense of insecurity, politicians find themselves having to speak to both aspects of how we live our lives, to both (in)security and the quest for at-homeness. In the interest of public knowledge, they have to inform the American public of potential or possible threats; they also have to say, "Don't worry, it'll be alright, go back to living your lives as you did before." This tension between protecting against threats and making the world a place to be at home in plagues us all, making it difficult to recreate a sense of normalcy and ordinariness. September 11 showed us that some events, regardless of how much we believe we are insulated from them or how far-fetched they might sound, can happen to any of us anywhere, anytime. We are not only in a world where predictability, trust, and security are in question. We are in a world where unpredictability, suspicion, and insecurity have become new watchwords and represent new challenges for the 21st century.

UNPREDICTABILITY

As 9-11 showed, unpredictability is a key element in terrorist strategy. Terrorists want to make sure that no one knows what is coming. This multiplies exponentially the impact of their attacks. There are few, if any, secrets about the array of tools of terror—various kinds of bombs and biological, chemical, or nuclear weapons. What we do not know, but need to know, is where, when, and how—uncertainties that have a pervasive impact on our daily lives. This unpredictability is designed to keep us off-guard, living under a cloud of uncertainty.

Part of the logic behind establishing the Office for Homeland Security was to regain some element of predictability by coordinating intelligence findings in order to avert terrorist attacks and to make it possible for Americans to go back to some facsimile of pre-9-11 life. Meanwhile, the unpredictability of global affairs has been "brought home" to us, and it seeps into our everyday lives, in the way we feel about our surroundings, in our confidence in the infrastructure of services we rely on, and in deciding how to plan activities at work or leisure. Terrorism, as has become clear, is about the threat of attacks as much as about the actual attacks. It exacts multiple kinds of costs—economic, in the security measures that are taken; political, in the impacts of security measures on the basics of American civic life; and psychological, in the malaise we feel in not knowing what will happen or when. The terrorist threat and the consequent war on terrorism threaten and disrupt our everyday living.

Unpredictability affects our lives by forcing us to pay attention to actions we previously handled by rote. We can still feel fairly confident that strangers on the street will not turn on us. But will they go through the expected performance rituals? Do *we* look suspicious to them? Are there everyday things that we decide to change, such as not working or living in a towering building? Do we drive rather than fly on our next business or vacation trip? If we decide to fly, do we find ourselves eyeing fellow passengers with misgivings? Do we hold back talking to the passenger next to us? Or do we take pains to check them out? Do we stay on alert, instead of napping or reading a favorite mystery novel? In one situation after another, we are liable to find ourselves questioning the basic elements of everyday actions, in part because we have lost the ability to take them completely for granted.

SUSPICION

The unpredictability that became more manifest after September 11 makes us pay more attention to the people we encounter and to our surroundings. What happens to our feelings about strangers when we read about terrorists who blended into our community and became invisible? What happens when we hear warnings that we must be suspicious of everything and everyone, ranging from our mail to "people who are not for us"? Just as unpredictability makes its way from the societal level into our daily lives, so does suspicion. The fact that the people who planned and executed the September 11 attacks lived among us and became part of our daily lives can prompt us to look at outsiders with suspicion. We find ourselves asking, What if?, a reaction fueled by dramatic media coverage of violence in unexpected places—a school, a post office, a factory. We expect our neighbors to be "like us" and treat our interactions with them as unmarked, until something goes horribly wrong. Then we tend toward a suspicious view of other people and become sensitive to "signs" that they might be a threat.

The 9-11 attacks opened the way to a level of suspicion characterized as "the fear of the other." Whether characterized as racism, ethnocentrism, or failure to understand other cultures, the fact that the attackers were Muslims and of Arab descent directed suspicion toward that particular group. It becomes another chapter in the tendency to fear and/or resent immigrants, a reaction that crops up in all countries—America included. The 9-11 attacks transformed fear of others into incidents involving harassment of and attacks on people of the Muslim faith or of Arabic or Sikh descent (because they all wear turbans, as one distorted rationale stated.). As terror-induced suspicion spilled over into suspicion of people who differed from mainstream Americans in their faith or ethnicity, the spillover was felt even by those who disagreed with U.S. foreign policy. If Americans were to fear that acting on two of the fundamental elements of American civic life—acceptance of immigrants and freedom of speech—would subject them to suspicion, this would represent another victory for 9-11 terrorists. We must be careful of viewing those who are different, either by background or by opinion, as suspect and in the extreme as siding with terrorists. The politics of suspicion is a difficult fight, resulting in people turning on one another. This is precisely what terrorism as a tactic is about: destroying the fabric of a society by getting the members of that society to tear it apart for them.

INSECURITY AND AFTER

The combination of unpredictability and suspicion creates another feeling—insecurity. What we confronted after 9-11 is the reality that everyday life in America did not operate in the way we thought it did. We were not *really* secure and living in predictable times. We found out that the security we assumed we had was not there. Insecurity came to the fore. When that happens, it is both natural and understandable to try to do something about it—to try to pursue *real* security.

So how do we reclaim that sense of being at home in a world where airplanes can become bombs, where U.S. troops wander through the desert looking for professional soldiers and terrorists who look like anonymous civilians, and where we no longer know whom to trust, whether it is our neighbor or our supposed political ally?

What we need, then, is to work on coming to terms with and creating a new at homeness in this new world social order, where unpredictability and suspicion reign. This social order is not one that can be controlled by one government or leader. Events in this new version of our world are only sporadically within anyone's clear control, and everyone must deal with the events, their causes, our responsibilities, and the ramifications of all these issues. This project is not something that the American government, no matter how hard it tries, can do for us on its own, nor is it a goal that we can achieve on our own. Instead, it is a symbiotic process that requires both the government and the American public to rethink how we live in the world. This is not to say that we need to explore such great ideological questions as, Is capitalism evil? or Is the U.S. an imperial power? Instead, we need to examine how we live our everyday lives. (*The roles of government, politics, leadership, and foreign policy are discussed elsewhere in this* book. Here, the discussion focuses on our experiences as individuals, "feeling our way.")

By working to create a sense of being at home instead of working only to maintain our security, we can rebuild the trust that is necessary if we are going to restore everydayness in our daily lives. That is not only the trust we have in strangers not attacking us or in the support our loved ones provide. It also needs to be an effort to rebuild trust as both an individual and a collective effort. That trust needs to be made explicit; we need to be able to say to those around us, "I trust you to be my neighbors," so that they can say the same to us. Think of how we talk about former friends or lovers, strangers, people who are different from us, or even the government and watch for the lack of trust that comes up in that discourse. Clearly, the creation of an explicitly given trust is necessary in the coming months and years. Trust brings predictability. Once we know for sure that we can trust others, we can predict what they will do and how they will conduct themselves. And this predictability reinforces the trust we place in others, which is what we need in order to feel secure—or rather, at home—in the world.

The difficulty, though, is that even before September 11, trust began disappearing from our world. As many social commentators, including Robert Putnam, have noted, there has been a breakdown over the past 50 years in our "civil society," the sphere of voluntary associations, informal interactions, and private circles of friends. Putnam's idea of "bowling alone"—pursuing activities individually that we used to do collectively—captures this sense perfectly. We no longer feel a part of our communities, our cities, or our nations, except in extreme circumstances. Even before 9-11, it had become clear that we needed to rebuild our trust in others and our sense of being at home in the world around us. September 11 has just made that clearer and showed us that the lack of community feeling does not simply stop at the borders of our neighborhood. It transcends the borders of our nation.

How do we embark on this project? How can we work to remake our world so we can feel at home, trust in others, have that trust reciprocated, and reclaim the kind of predictability that makes it possible to live a safe and secure life? As already indicated, it is a symbiotic process, one that requires both our involvement and that of our government. While that might seem to be an impossible task, given the position our government finds itself in, we can engage in the process with personal involvement that, in and of itself, will add to our own sense of security.

We can begin by making it clear to elected officials that politics of suspicion and insecurity are unacceptable to *us*, thereby making them unpalatable to elected officials. Democracy or not, our government primarily relies on one thing for determining its political agenda: opinion polls. If the American people make it clear that these kinds of politics are not acceptable, such politics can change, apocalyptic rhetoric cease, and new ways of thinking about America's relationship with the world appear. We may be part of the war on terrorism, but it has not been a long-standing war, though critics argue that it could very well last indefinitely, giving rise to continued politics of suspicion and insecurity. So why not bring about a "war on suspicion," one that could allay the conditions that stand in the way of living comfortably at home with others?

In our own lives, we need to find ways to rethink how we live near and with others. Are we maintaining a bunker mentality or are we actually getting to know others? Are we clinging to a Cold War mantra, "America—love it or leave it"? Or are we discussing with others across political, social, economic, and cultural/ethnic boundaries how we can individually and collectively bring about a new America? Is our reaction to September 11 and those who perpetrated it being generalized to everyone with similar ethnic and religious backgrounds? Are we able to separate the criminals from "the others"? It is not terrorists who might destroy the American way; it is we as Americans who will make or break the American way of life in the 21st century. It is up to us in the way we respond to the attacks of 9-11, in the way we define ourselves, in the ways in which we think about ourselves as individual Americans dealing positively with the human condition, and in the choices we make about how we will live with others in the world, both near and afar.

3

RENEWING OUR WAYS OF THINKING

But we are all seekers. We all want to know why....a story without end, as we continue to explore our humanity in the eternal Why. And we see how we have come from seeking meaning to finding meaning in the seeking.

HISTORIAN DANIEL J. BOORSTIN

At a previously obscure safety supply company in Long Island City across from Manhattan, New Yorkers lined up in pursuit of safety after 9-11. They "besieged" the supplier (as reported by a *New Yorker* magazine reporter), selecting and buying gloves, suits for chemical spills, respirators, and gas masks. At one extreme of anxiety, a woman customer asked, "Do you have masks for dogs?" At the other extreme—life-as-usual—the warehouse manager dismissed an obvious question about whether the company's employees had safety gear themselves. "Of course not. You can't live your life worrying about that sort of thing."

After 9-11, Americans shaped their responses to the threat of terror, mostly within these two extremes of doing something (almost anything) and of resigning themselves to what happens. Each of us is practicing real-life epistemology, identifying the reality that is out there, which exists whether or not we like it, know it, or acknowledge it. We normally live—more unconsciously than consciously— according to what we have decided is the world around us, including the odds-on risks and how much risk we can tolerate. One person's fear of flying is another person's routine commuter flight. For some people, an elevator ride is a convenient alternative to the stairs; for others, it's a frightening trip in a claustrophobic space. Some people fear open spaces; others fear closed places. Phobias of all kinds and the fears they trigger are common knowledge and painful experiences. What is new are the expanded ranks of people worrying about risks they once dismissed as far-fetched and the growing number of things to worry about, phobias aside. The boundaries between normal and neurotic, between far-fetched fears and sensible precautions, have changed dramatically. We are revising our ways of thinking about the world around us.

In making us all practicing epistemologists, the war on terrorism makes us all odds makers who decide what is acceptable risk (driving at 70 miles an hour), what is a far-fetched risk (driving to the supermarket), what risks to avoid (white-water rafting, rappelling off a mountainside). "What if?" thinking has become a national pastime. What could be next, what can we guard against, as individuals and as a nation? Our answers are not in a steady state, depending on whether we worked near the Twin Towers, knew someone who did, had planned to attend a client meeting in one of the upper floors, how much TV coverage we watch, and the latest terrorist incident/threat/warning. Or whether we are an American Airlines pilot responsible for a planeload of passengers and skeptical of the credentials belonging to an Arab-American passenger who is a member of the President's personal security detail. After questioning by the pilot, airline officials, and airport police, the agent was denied passage, even though he had offered to have the Secret Service confirm his identity. After 9-11, the incident is believable, rather than bizarre, as the dividing line between the improbable and possible tilts toward more, rather than less caution.

Terrorism at our doorstep forces each of us to confront the realities of the danger behind threats and terrorist intentions—to our country, our city or town, our neighborhood, our home, ourselves, others. The more threatened that we feel, the more likely it is that we prefer to be "safe rather than sorry." Many of us go further, doing something, almost anything, even when we realize it offers little protection. Let us not discount psychological comfort. It feels "real." Like the woman at the safety supply company who spent $1,109.13 on safety equipment, even though she doubted its efficacy or that it would be used. "I just want to feel like I did whatever I could to protect my family."

WEIGHING THE ODDS

The many-sided, multidirectional threats of terrorism force Americans to weigh the odds and rethink their attitude to dangers they may face. For one thing, it depends on how we calculate the odds and what odds are acceptable when we weigh risk against degree of probability, danger against the need to go on with our lives, the peril against the price to be paid if the law of averages catches up with us. For each of us, the threshold of defensive behavior and initiatives is different, somewhere at and between the extremes of nervous New Yorkers shopping or ignoring safety equipment. Depending on how suspicious or sensitive we are, we risk more or less embarrassment, more or less adverse reactions if we disrupt the people around us in pursuit of safety. Some of us will hesitate, others speak up to demand to disembark just after boarding a jumbo jet and noticing a "suspicious" person on board. What about reporting to the FBI that "Arabic-looking" visitors are coming and going to a neighbor's house? What we think and how we identify danger are variable reactions, no doubt reaching back to parental influence and childhood experiences, even to how tall or short, thin or stout we are, even to our birth order.

Socrates would have us start our thinking process within ourselves, in line with the bedrock Delphic advice, *know thyself*. In 21st-century America, we propose starting with a close look at the outside world. To get anywhere near our inner world, we need to clear a path through the avalanche of distractions and daily duties that constitute lives dominated by "busyness." We need to recover from a day of overwork (a common complaint) and withstand the assault on our senses and competition for our attention from family, friends, the media, the mail, the phone, the community, the pile of bills. We can, of course, turn off the TV, but give all the many channels credit. They know how to get our attention and to keep us tuned in. They know how to make events into daily dramas, to mix news and entertainment into both an enlightening and distracting experience. They know that violence, the bizarre, the shocking, the sensational, and the scandalous draw audiences. Just look at circulation and ratings. In the final analysis, they give us what we want.

The media mentality is illustrated by the reaction of a high-powered TV news director when a magazine writer once asked to observe and describe the daily production of his market-leading six o'clock show. He refused the attention, however ego-nourishing, and for good reason. Out of context, the rules of competitive journalism can seem appalling: The more casualties, the better; the more footage of blood and gore, the better the story for the top of the show; the "worse" the news, the "better." The news director did not want to go public with news judgment—discussions of the story lineup and decisions on news value. His reporters, writers, and producers were not cold-blooded and calloused. They were chasing audience. It's their job.

On our end as audience, life in a news and information-saturated society takes effort if we want to avoid the coach potato stereotype. We cannot leave it to the stream of media to keep things in perspective. They will give us what we want and demand (as we demonstrate by the newspapers and magazines each of us read, the TV we watch, the movies we go to see or rent). In the final analysis, making sense of news and information is up to us. We must withstand invasions on our emotions by the media vying for and getting our attention and by their passion for celebrities (who basically, as noted by historian Daniel Boorstin, are famous for being famous). It can even damage our health to pay too much attention to what's happening in an increasingly dangerous world, as therapists found in the wake of 9-11 and prescribed tranquilizers. Family doctors have had the same experience, such as the practitioner who shakes his head in dismay when describing the case of a hale and hearty 80-year-old who precipitously went downhill as TV watching began to do him in. He could not turn off the upsetting and disturbing TV coverage of Ground Zero. He was tied to the set as though it were a life-support system, but it was quite the opposite.

In trying to reach inside ourselves and to focus on what really matters for us as individuals living our lives and as citizens participating in our society, we have an accumulation of clutter to clear away or at least cope with. On the way to an examined life, we must take control of our lives amidst the litter. It is not only a matter of "finding the time." It is a matter of paying attention—of living, feeling, and responding within the moment and of coming into contact with our real selves. We have to scrape away the barnacles of busy lives and the distractions of a consumer society. The effort is not limited to overworked executives and managers, whose hands are fuller than ever and who are in danger of burning out. Americans live busy lives in a busy country. Our children are well trained for a future as viewers and consumers. They qualify as the world's busiest, most categorized, most stimulated youngsters, targets of the best marketing efforts money can buy. Yes, broad brush strokes run the risk of caricature, but they do paint a recognizable backdrop to mindsets shaken up by terror.

A time of uncertainty puts ingrained attitudes on the spot in confronting a new normalcy. In reaching for equilibrium, we must think twice about our attitudes and enter consciously (and uncomfortably) into a personal campaign of adjustment and rethinking. Of course, change does signal opportunities, but only with eyes wide open to the impact of what is happening. Compared with yesterday, what is today really like? Back to back, today and yesterday, how different are our lives, our hopes, our dreams? How different are our feelings? How do we change our way of thinking to deal with the changes we are forced to pay attention to? How do we tune into changes that are coming on strong while we never notice? The warning is familiar but still relevant: watch out for "future shock."

While reminders about a changing world are not new, close-to-home terrorism forces us to pay more attention than before. During the counter-cultural outburst of the 1960s, physicist J. Robert Oppenheimer made a comment that needs no updating and deserves a ready nod of acknowledgment: "One thing that is new is the prevalence of newness, the changing scale and scope of change itself, so that the world alters as we walk in it." Terrorism is a blood-soaked finger pointing toward change as a basic component of our human condition, with its uncompromising rule of life and death. As the philosopher Heraclitus reminded ancient Greeks in his historic admonition, we "cannot step twice into the same river." It's a dangerous mistake to think we can.

Terrorists, as they intended, shattered our comforting view that while the river may be moving and changing, we are still here, we stand our ground, we are safe. It would be far-fetched to say that 9-11 on its own had an immediate, long-lasting, permanent impact. America did not completely change one traumatic Tuesday morning. We Americans were forced to pay attention to realities that were already changing the world, our world. Our portfolio of attitudes was put under serious pressure by our immediate reactions and sense of shock. In a time of adjustment, we can no longer hope to go home again to pre-9-11 comfort levels.

Whether it is job security, physical health, or safe streets, we are surrounded by ongoing threats that do not go away by denying their existence. We are hostages to fortune, though the American story has so many happy endings that it is easy to feel that we are immune to misfortune, even able to fight wars with hardly any casualties, and can count on having it better from one generation to the next. Up, up, and away feels great—until the bubble bursts. So we recommend against avoidance and urge factoring in the risk built into the human condition and the new normalcy, even in America.

Avoidance, aided, abetted, and facilitated by the distractions all around us, makes it possible to ignore changes and the emergence of new realities. There is nothing new about denial as a coping mechanism. Busyness—on the job, at play, with hobbies, in social activity, in the pursuit of pleasure—keeps us distracted, and the more we are immersed, the better we may even feel, until called to attention. Legal and illegal use of drugs reaches for better living through chemistry. Similar and healthy results are provided by a workout at the gym. Perspiration and anxiety do not cohabit. Once endorphin kicks in, we feel better, but only for the time being. Removing symptoms interrupts but does not remove anxiety. Enter terrorism, the dread reminder—the less realistic we have been, the greater the shock.

Rather than outright avoidance, it can make sense to take control of avoidance by locating where we stand on risk. What is the degree of risk that faces us? What can we realistically do to protect ourselves and others? What can we expect, and what should we demand from our local and national leadership? What responsibilities do we have as concerned individuals, citizens, parents, friends, neighbors, colleagues?

FIGURING OUT A RESPONSE

In responding to such issues, we recommend Blaise Pascal's celebrated "wager." The proposition of the 17th-century French philosopher focuses on belief in God, but can extend to all situations where people face uncertainty, where answers to serious questions are not unequivocal, where we are in the seeking, rather than finding mode. Pascal approached belief in God as a gamble on whether God exists. If so, then a believer can look forward to eternal life, while atheists can be viewed as hell-bound. So why not bet on God's existence? While we live, we have the comfort of that belief and the prospect of reward in the afterlife. If we lose the bet by believing, we lose nothing. If we win, we win big.

With adjustments (and without detouring into a theoretical discussion), we propose thinking of the Pascal wager as a useful way to view terrorism and the myriad threats that we can think of and those we cannot. We can live assuming that "it won't happen to me," while taking precautions that feel right. Specifically:

- Demand that those in power do everything constitutional and necessary to protect us. From Main Street to Pennsylvania Avenue, we can use the tried-and-tested methods of applying political pressure to local, state, and federal government in demanding responsible policies and actions.

- Stay informed, starting with the precautions recommended by official government agencies and supplemented by watchdog groups of experts.

- Avoid overreacting to individual episodes. The same media that do so well in keeping us up to date are event-driven. As noted, the latest and most dramatic are what journalists in all media live by. Their pursuit of headlines and of air time can distort our understanding of what is really important and misdirect our precautions against risks. Sometimes the risk is greater, sometimes less than it seems. Beware of headlines, which can function the way pickpockets do—attracting attention and distracting us while grabbing our wallet.

■ Take a positive attitude. Count on the law of averages to be in our favor, while taking into account what the government and we as individuals can do. That's in line with President Bush's urging that we go on with our lives. Americans showed every sign of getting his message. Six weeks after 9-11, a Gallup poll found that the percentage of Americans describing their mood as "good" had dropped by only five percentage points, compared with the previous January. Two-thirds were not "worried" about anthrax and thought there was no good reason to be afraid of terrorist threats.

■ Take a second look at our personal way of life and how we nourish body and mind. Here is where our information-rich environment can be a useful ally, replete with sound advice and guidance. From the Internet to newsletters, from magazine cover stories to specialized cable TV channels, there is a healthy diet of information and guidance available to all of us. It arrives from many directions, as in a thoughtful newsletter sent to readers of the University of California, Berkeley *Wellness Letter*. Referring to the post-9-11 "sense of vulnerability," Dr. John Swartzberg suggests "strategies to promote resiliency." His worthwhile reminders include following your regular routine and sticking to a healthy diet, remembering to turn off the TV occasionally, and trying to keep things in perspective. He reminds us that we need to give ourselves a breather, a change of pace, a walk in the woods, get-togethers with friends. He cites the need for "even a few laughs," something that he points out as "much needed these days." For good measure, he adds an optimistic reminder: "Also, don't forget that we Americans are a resourceful, durable and resilient people. We not only survived the horrors of World War II, but experienced unprecedented prosperity during the half century that followed."

■ Make adjustments that make sense, based on the best understanding of risk and our own risk tolerance. Often, inconvenience is more than risk as the factor that changes our behavior. It makes sense to take into account the difference between the two. The greater the security, the greater the inconvenience, and the more cooperation we must commit ourselves to providing.

What New York Senator Charles E. Schumer said about learning from 9-11 applies to us as individuals, as well as the government: "We live in a new world and everything has to be recalibrated." Depending on where we stand on the optimism/pessimism continuum, "recalibration" will vary for all of us as individuals. In line with our discussion of Pascal's gamble, we are partial to an optimistic outlook. It not only feels better but appears more realistic, in view of not only the long odds against terrorism striking us directly, but also of our tremendous national assets, global support, and determination to prevail.

Recalibration of how uncertainty impacts our lives is an individual and rough calculation to make in conjunction with all the other people in our lives and in terms of responsibilities and goals. Whatever the calculation, we must face the fact that the greater our vulnerability (real or perceived), the less control we have or can take over at least some of our lives. We face trade-off situations between what we want to do and what we can do in changed circumstances, between what we must do and what must be done to make it possible, between what we add to our activities and what we subtract. As part of making any plans, how much should security figure in? This involves what we do, what others do, what those in charge of security require. Our portfolio of time, energy, and effort needs to be reexamined and changed accordingly. Here, for example, is how rethinking can affect planning, arranging and conducting activities.

TIME

Our control over time and timing is under pressure. Standard security procedures and unexpected disruptions can interfere with or disrupt any of our activities. We cannot be as certain as in the past of timetables, schedules, and commitments. In conducting personal and company business, how much time will it take? How do new rules and procedures complicate matters?

TRAVEL

In a country dependent on air travel, a trip to the nearest airport illustrates the changed travel picture. How much extra time do we need to allow for check-in? What are the prospects for extra delays from security false alarms and from tie-ups in other airports? What am I carrying on my person or in my luggage that will raise an alarm? How much more time will it take to make a trip, whether by car, bus, train, or plane? What happens in any form of travel, even going downtown, if security needs disrupt normal activities? Americans will hesitate leaving home without a cell phone (already a staple item for people of all ages). Whether traveling for business or pleasure, domestic or foreign destinations, which airline should we take, which countries and airports have optimum and efficient security, which have the best track records for security, the most efficiency?

INFRASTRUCTURE

Given the priority on security, what are the possible disruptions in public services, ranging from water, gas, and electricity to calls for emergency assistance? What goods and services will unexpectedly face shortages? If and when terrorist attacks occur or are threatened, what disruptions will result? If we need vaccines or other health supplies, will they be readily available when needed? Should we stock up on bottled water, flashlights, canned food? If we cannot get home from work or need to stay out overnight, what backup arrangements are called for?

DOING BUSINESS

Since "time is money" in an advanced economy, delay is costly, disruption potentially disastrous. Can we count on other businesses that we work with to come through? Are they at risk to terror, to the vagaries of the marketplace? Inside our companies, can we count on out-of-town participants to make it to meetings? How do we adjust to no-shows? When and where are the best venues for major meetings? Should we even hold a general meeting? What contingency planning is called for in case of a disaster? What logistics are involved? What are the costs?

THE CHALLENGE OF KNOWING THYSELF

Beyond such practical issues, which we can accommodate at a price in time, money, and effort, what about the fundamental issue of *know thyself*? How do we approach life as individuals, define our place in the world, ponder who we are and what we want to be? This means thinking about our ways of thinking, a process in which we can benefit from all the help we can get. Any such confrontation can have an uncomfortable undercurrent: What am I becoming? Is this what I want to become? What is my life all about? How do I feel about myself, really feel?

Two enlightening person-to-person conversations illustrate what is involved in this process—one with a widely acclaimed voice of reason and humanism from the last century, the other with a psychologist who has a national following for her work in addressing the mind/body connection. Highlights of the conversations provide reminders and insights that can serve us all in renewing our ways of thinking. First, there is Joan Borysenko, Ph.D., president of Mind/Body Health Sciences in Boulder, Colorado, who draws on her work as scientist, therapist, and consultant. Here is her view of the optimism/pessimism divide:

> Any shocking event reveals our thinking, whether we're going to be resilient and transformed by difficulty, whether we think like an optimist or a pessimist. It shows in how we think when something rocks our world. There are people who feel like life is over and that things will never be the same, people who are less likely to see possible opportunities. Then you have another group of people who say it's difficult, it's terrible. I have grief, I have sadness, I have fear. I also see that it opens up totally new

ways of thinking and possibly new ways of reprioritizing my life. Now that I recognize that life is inherently uncertain, I can see what life really means to me. I can live more in the moment. I can see how I can be of better service to the world. So the larger question is how one responds during a dark night of the soul. In a certain way, suffering is a lesson because it sloughs complacency. It would be safe to say what's most important to human beings would be finding that center of peace and compassion within ourselves and the wisdom of creativity so that we live a life in service to others.

Because Borysenko traveled extensively during the weeks after 9-11 (some 50 different flights), she is in an unusual position to gauge the immediate responses of Americans coast to coast. Her findings were not unexpected.

Underlying grief and uncertainty. . . . It took the slightest reminder for people to burst into tears. They share their fears for the future, certainly their fears for their children. At the same time, people have been mobilized in a big response—if not now, when; if not you, who?

It's very clear that some people are having trouble coping. One of the other things, besides optimism/pessimism, is the basic stress levels in their lives. If someone is already at the edge of what they can bear, it doesn't take a whole lot to push them over the edge. The more general stress we take out of our lives, the better are our coping reserves for dealing with a truly extraordinary challenge like 9-11.

Borysenko argues convincingly that America's "coping reserves" were already low before 9-11. She points to an "anxious and worried culture" and describes Americans as a nation that has "never been wealthier—or more miserable." Americans, she adds, are struggling to achieve what Borysenko calls the "inner peace that makes life worth living." While the struggle is waged by Americans as individuals, cumulatively, the effort is massive, as exemplified by spending on self-help books alone, which reached $563 million in the year 2000. Sales of such books and the Bible surged after 9-11, a sure sign of greater do-it-yourself efforts to achieve mental balance and a sense of well-being. Cold, hard industry data supports Borysenko's dispiriting reminder about our culture after a decade of soaring prosperity:

- About one in three Americans is sleep deprived, with complaints of exhaustion and trouble holding things together.

- Visits to doctors' offices for anxiety increased by 31 percent between 1990 and 1997; visits for panic disorder more than doubled.

- More than one in five Americans is depressed or has chronic "low mood."

- 70 to 90 percent of visits to primary care physicians is attributed to stress.

This unforgiving data tracks the efforts of Americans to come to terms with who we are as we think about ourselves and the world we live in. As someone widely praised for her work in helping others with stress, spirituality, and the mind/body connection, Borysenko speaks to the challenge of coping with the post-9-11 world. Hers is a voice of optimism tempered by realism:

> From the viewpoint of our material and physical safety, there is a very, very, very great threat. From a totally different point of view, I would say the opportunity has never been greater to grow as human beings, to grow in terms of our connection with one another, in our understanding of what's important in life, in our commitment to service and to our relationship with God. I would say that my greatest sustenance and the place where I find God most evident is in the love that I share with a very wise circle of friends. Then, of course, I find quite a lot of sustenance in prayer and meditation, in my dogs that I love and in beauty, in nature, in things that grow.

A flashback to a memorable conversation taped with the influential 20th-century voice of humanism, the late Erich Fromm, recalls the distinction he made between the "having" mode, centered around things and property, and the "being" mode, which is centered around persons. His advice is to look at ourselves: "Analyze your own *having* tendencies—having prestige, possessions, one's jealousy, one's greed. Those tendencies are usually unconscious and need analyzing." He recommended an hour every morning in self-analysis and meditation. While we may not find the suggestion of a daily 60 minutes feasible or realistic, Fromm was clearly pointing in the direction of knowing ourselves in the Biblical tradition of looking beyond the material and reaching for the spiritual.

Literally a child of his century—born in 1900—Fromm influenced generations of thoughtful Americans with his writing on love, hope, psychoanalysis, and human nature. For him, the difference that mattered was not between believers and unbelievers but between those who cared about religious questions and those who didn't. While his background and upbringing undoubtedly shaped him, it never defined him. A practicing Orthodox Jew (until age 26), he characterized himself as a non-theist. He was a renowned psychoanalyst, author, and teacher. Two of his books became landmarks on humanism: *The Art of Loving* and *The Revolution of Hope.* His outlook, as described in a memorable meeting with one of this book's authors, spoke to life in any time of uncertainty, even if "the chances for our survival are very, very small." (At the time, Fromm said it was "maybe five percent, two percent.")

When asked whether he was a pessimist or optimist, Fromm rejected either label. What emerges is a two-sided self-image of someone who was "a peculiar mixture of pessimist and optimist." He characterized himself "as a man who has a deep faith in love." At the age of 76 (four years before his death), he was clearly a man who would never give up, who faced up to what he identified as the human condition—part of nature and subject to its laws, but also transcending it by virtue of self-awareness and reason. For him, what counted was loving, nonexploitive effort on behalf of personal well-being, humanist that he was. The odds, as pessimistic as he saw them, never overcame an abiding commitment never to give up.

> As long as there is life I cannot give up hope. As long as one could not prove that there is no way of hope, as long as that is the case, I shall have faith in life. That's not a matter of computers and of calculations. It's a deep faith in life and I have written about some factors which support somewhat this rationally. But I separate very definitely my realistic reasoning in which my emotions are not participating from my feeling which says everything must be done as long as there is a possibility. And the two don't conflict with each other because as long as there is a possibility, even a small one, then everything must be done to save life.

Like Fromm, Borysenko speaks to a common denominator of love and of reaching out for it, working at it. They are two among the many thought leaders concerned about "religious questions," viewed in the broadest sense. Whatever differences in what they believe, they share the tradition of *know thyself* and a have a common starting point—inside our individual selves.

Borysenko: "I do think that any tragedy like this has to make you look inward to your most deeply held values and ask, What am I doing here?" What's the definition of a life well-lived or finding the definition of success? For me, what it's come down to after all these years is that the definition is to give and receive love, to reflect our beautiful world with gratitude back to the Creator. When that thing (9-11) happens, the good fallout is that everywhere you travel, people talk to strangers, there is a sense of wanting to be tied to other people. I've never felt more community, more sense of service, of love, of togetherness everywhere. These are really spiritual values and experiences they're talking about. That's always been the case. Disaster tends to bring out these things that seem important to people."

Fromm: "The constant development of love and non-hate is the only way to mental health. There is none other. Whether this is phrased in Christian theological terms or not, that is a very secondary question to me. What matters to me is the kind of life a person leads or wants to lead or struggles to lead, what he or she really considers sin. I believe mental health can only be reached in this way. People who lose their souls, who are scattered, who chase after the manifoldness of things with the drives that come from the manifoldness of their desires are people who lose themselves. They have no center, no selves. They necessarily have to build their security on greed, on all the things that make people unhappy."

Borysenko: "From the point of view of our material and physical safety, there is a very, very great threat. From a totally different point of view, the opportunities have never been greater to grow as human beings, to grow in terms of our connections with one another, to understand what's important in life, to grow in our relationship with God."

PESSIMISM VERSUS OPTIMISM

Thinking in terms of personal renewal brings us face to face with a continuum of inner feeling and outlook. On the dark side, are we caught up in depression and anxiety? Or are we on the bright side, looking forward to the day, feeling the joy of living? We propose taking a cue from an illuminating approach set forth by the perceptive psychologist and author, Lawrence LeShan. In his book *Alternative Realities* (New York: Ballantine Books, 1977), he points to the "central idea" that "we human beings invent reality as much as we discover it," and that "if this is comprehended, we have a wide choice as to how we invent it and therefore, what sort of world we live in."

Whether we call the continuum that we invent/discover as pessimism to optimism or dark side to bright side, we know the differences when we see them. Based on common sense and 9-11 observations, here is our description:

PESSIMISM/DARK SIDE

Pessimists, who proverbially see the glass as half empty, look mainly for what's wrong, expect the worst, come up with What If? formulations which lead to negative expectations. They are most comfortable finding what's wrong, so that's where they look first in seeking what won't and can't work. They tend to mistrust others and downplay the prospects of positive results. Typical responses: "It hasn't worked in the past." "What makes you think anything's going to change?" They take a narrow view of possibilities and would rather not try. They magnify setbacks, minimize positive results. They are quick to criticize, slow to praise. They get up each day on the wrong side of the bed.

OPTIMISM/BRIGHT SIDE

Optimists, seeing the glass as half-filled, look mainly for what's right, expect the best, come up with What If? formulations which lead to positive expectations. They are most comfortable seeing what's right, so that's where they look first in seeking what will and can work. Typical responses: "What have we done in the past that's worked?" "What do we have going for us?" "What can I do?" They take the widest view of possibilities, open to answers from any and all directions. They are ready to try anything. They minimize any setbacks, magnify positive results. They are quick to praise, slow to criticize. They get up each day on the right side of the bed.

Over the years, watching young men and women plan and begin careers, observing colleagues, comparing those who do well with their lives with those who don't, we can safely stand behind an upbeat generalization: Optimists have a far better winning record than do pessimists. They expect positive things and achieve them more often than pessimists. They also have more energy to devote to their activities, fueled by the expectation that what they do will make a difference. Certainly, they smile more often and are more appealing to have around. So as a result, we "reward" them. We are more likely to support their efforts, to see them as top performers, to join forces with them. One undeniable sign is in the workplace, where there is no doubt that optimists make the best sellers of goods and services, as well as their own abilities. This is confirmed in the world of teaming, from the schoolyard to the boardroom, where optimists are the teammates of choice.

Particularly important, optimists feel as though they are in charge of their lives and, therefore, feel better about themselves and the world. There are no secrets to joining their ranks. We can begin by listening to sound advice all around us and by taking charge of our own thinking and feeling. What Fromm and Borysenko advise, from one generation to another, from one century to the next, never becomes obsolete if, as we believe, human nature and the human condition basically never change. Of course, the mechanics of living, thanks to technology, change dramatically, but not the basic issues of finding our place in the world and making a life.

At a time like this, tried-and-true reminders are worth repeating:

- Take responsibility for our inner lives by paying attention to the thoughts and feelings that shape our outlook.
- Work on balancing our personal/family/work/play lives.
- Activate the age-old concept of the Sabbath/Sunday, thereby setting apart time that is devoted to ourselves. No work. No chores. No shopping. Full time-outs, regularly.
- Get in close touch with other people and listen to what they have to say.
- Help others. Those who do so also help themselves.
- Bring variety into life with exploratory reading, a new hobby or interest, hearing a lecture, taking a course, learning a new skill, taking up painting, learning to play an instrument.
- Enjoy ourselves in positive and enriching ways. To each his or her own version.
- Take care of both body and soul and never stop paying attention to what that means.

We are on the side of those who advise taking charge of our lives and ourselves, and we argue that doing so moves us into the ranks of optimists, who are by definition proactive, rather than reactive. Pessimists are the opposite. They are primarily reactive, taking action as a last resort, typically when it is too late to make a difference.

LOOKING TO THE FUTURE

In renewing our way of thinking, one dimension deserves particular attention: a mindset of looking to the future. A hallmark of the American psyche and of optimists in general, the power of this orientation was confirmed in studies of Nazi concentration camp survivors. Researchers found in case after case the will to live, determination to overcome immediate problems and hardships, and something else. Survivors tended to look to the future. They devoted considerable mental energy to thinking about what they would do after the horrible chapter of their lives in a concentration camp. One man thought about writing a book on history, another about teaching music, and so it went, each with his or her own particular vision. The details of a future vision did not matter. What mattered was having a vision.

This combination of faith and hope is a basic coping technique in tough times. It recalls the survivor mentality of American POWs from World War II, Korea, and Vietnam, who cited the value of looking to the future. It places the present in perspective and gives hope its best chance. The real *you*, the important *you*, the *you* singled out by Bory-senko and Fromm cannot be touched by the enemy. It is inside us. We are in charge of our mind, our attitudes, and our spirit. This realization is an essential part of coping with the stress and hardship of the *new normalcy*. It addresses the reality that in life there are good and bad times, and what counts is how we face up to both. The English poet William Blake crystallized this fact of life with a rhymed reminder, "Man was made for Joy & Woe/And when this we rightly know/Thro(ugh) the World we safely go."

In these tough times, when we are in an economic recession on top of fighting a war against terrorism, we can draw on the strength of the national psyche, as well as our own psychological resources. Looking to the future does not mean ignoring today's realities and escaping into future dreams; it means mixing attitude and action with sound priorities. In a country like ours, realistic optimism enshrines confidence in a better tomorrow that all Americans work for. In turning toward the bright side, we focus our thoughts and feelings on positives in the life at hand, on what the positives mean to us, and what we can mean to others. With such a focus, we celebrate the day as it begins and honor the day that was. It is part of finding our way— in life and at work—as we pursue opportunities and personal rewards beyond the reach of terrorism. It is a quintessentially American response in a nation whose history is a parable of incorrigible optimism. It is a matter of finding our way at work, the arena in which we spend most of our time and energy.

4

FINDING OUR WAY AT WORK

The times they are a-changin'.

BOB DYLAN

During World War II, the government created a large bureaucracy to control the price of almost everything sold in the United States. Controls included the use of all raw materials, allocating them first for military purposes. Just about anything in the marketplace—all types of metals, nuts and bolts, wiring, food, and chemicals—came under government control. If a company wanted to manufacture a product, it had to get permission to do so, and if granted permission, it was told how many it could make. Many products not deemed crucial to the war effort were banned, with officials not allowing them to be manufactured. If you ran a company that made airplanes or guns, things were terrific, but if you made cash registers, government regulations forbade these to be made at all (the metal was needed for the war effort). You were out of business. Right? Wrong. But you did have a big problem to solve.

That was the challenge facing the National Cash Register Company (NCR), one of the most distinguished companies in America and the giant of the cash register business, as dominant then as Microsoft is today with PC software. In today's stock market, the news that NCR could not make any cash registers would make it look like a very bad dot-com gone very wrong. To be sure, the company protested and scrambled to create whole new product lines for the war effort, from bomb sights to aircraft components to deciphering equipment. At the same time, NCR stayed in the cash register market, turning what looked like a disaster into a tale of opportunity-seeking and survival.

Once senior management realized that government contracts would barely keep the company alive and certainly could not preserve the core business which had made the firm a success since the 1880s, it looked for a way out of the crisis. To grow its business, the company needed cash registers that it could rent. So it went all over the world, buying every second-hand NCR register it could lay its hands on, shipped them to its main factory in Dayton, Ohio, and rebuilt them. NCR refurbished machines manufactured as far back as the 1890s, cannibalizing machines for parts and metal. Reconditioned machines were then rented as NCR had always done. The firm made money, maintained its skills in the manufacture of cash registers, and retained its customers. No new models were introduced during the war, but after the fighting ended, along with price and production controls, NCR launched new products, made at its Dayton factory and leased to its surviving core of customers. When NCR war veterans returned home, they had jobs waiting in a company that had converted crisis into opportunity.

In the late 1990s, a once-endangered Japanese motorcycle maker celebrated another version of opportunity-driven survival and success. On March 27, 1997, Honda celebrated the tenth anniversary of becoming America's first Japanese luxury import marque, having come a long way from its own prospects after World War II. Honda's distinctive capability became its ticket to success: building efficient engines at low cost. So the company went into the car business, with motors made by Honda and practically everything else outsourced. It became a formidable player in the U.S. car marketplace with its trademark engines in cars with standard features selling at premium prices. Often cited as a model for the future organization, Honda reduced the amount of time from design to production of an automobile to one year, when the typical U.S. firm was taking seven years. In the automobile industry, Honda became a leader in fuel efficiency and low-emission technology. Only eight years after putting the Acura on the market through 60 dealers, the car reached one million sales. On its tenth anniversary, the company had 270 car dealers selling its cars and, for good measure, 50 different motorcycle models and variations.

In both examples, the two companies faced up to change in the marketplace by figuring out what they confronted and what they could do about it. In viewing the knowledge and the skills they had as organizations, they looked for what was relevant to the marketplace in terms of the present and the future, not the past. As oil tycoon J. Paul Getty once pointed out, "There are always opportunities through which businessmen can profit handsomely if they will only recognize and seize them." The new normalcy doesn't change the formula for success: Look for opportunities which are all around us, figure out how to leverage our resources, and remain flexible in matching what the organization can do with what the marketplace wants. The search should never stop in either the best or worst of times. In the changing times we face, it can be a matter of survival.

WHAT THE NEW NORMALCY MEANS FOR BUSINESS

The new normalcy highlights basic business issues: what new operational implications now exist, what opportunities are emerging to grow markets and sales, what is going away, what is likely to emerge. As demanding as the questions are, there are attitudes and trends that can point the way to plausible answers. Approaching change with an open mind to possibilities and dangers has long governed the actions of savvy business leaders. The approach that succeeds in dealing with changing circumstances centers on optimizing circumstances. As stated by the legendary coach of the Green Bay Packers, Vince Lombardi, "The spirit, the will to win," and "the will to excel are the things that endure." In difficult and uncertain times, there's no avoiding the tried-and-true strategy of focusing on basic values. Peter F. Drucker argues that "concentration is the key to economic results." So, too, are leadership, an open mind, calmness of purpose, and determination to weather tough times, and perhaps most of all right now, applying problem-solving techniques.

In the first two months following 9-11, the business community in the United States, and to a similar but lesser extent, in Europe suffered a tremendous shock. The U.S. GDP in the third quarter, already weak, shrank. Many businesses saw sales volumes near zero in the first week after the bombings and only slowly began to increase over the next two months, without reaching pre-9-11 levels. In the U.S., over 500,000 people lost their jobs in the six weeks following 9-11. Stock markets around the world shrank instantly in value by almost 15 percent. In October, when

companies reported their third quarter earnings and signaled the market on the next quarter's prospects, the news
was dismal in almost every industry. If we were to judge
events by conditions as they existed in late 2001, we could
easily decide that the best thing to do was to buy gold and
drop out.

But that would not be the whole story. It has been
America's long experience that all wars profoundly stimulate its economy, while at the same time changing in many
ways how work is done. New opportunities present themselves and eventually outweigh the negatives while—yes—
many old practices and business opportunities shrink.
NCR's experience during and after World War II illustrates
all these elements at work. And it is happening again.

The American government, which had set its course on
shrinking expenditures before 9-11 and, indeed, had
refunded taxes to the public, did a complete reversal in the
first 45 days after the terrorist attacks. With nearly light-
ning speed, the Congress passed a $40 billion package to
fund the initial round of expenses for waging war against
terrorism and to provide financial relief for airline companies, which particularly suffered in the aftermath of the
hijackings and bombings. As it became clearer in the fall
that the economy had moved into recession, signaled by
the very sharp increase in the number of unemployed, the
U.S. government began to design an even larger stimulus
package than the initial $40 billion. If someone had asked a

member of the Republican administration six months earlier whether they could ever imagine asking Congress to spend over $140 billion on stimulating the economy and pushing the government into deficit spending, they would have said, "No way, not in a million years." But that all changed after 9-11.

If the past is any indication of things to come, most if not all the new stimulus money will be spent in the United States. Because it will be aimed at certain sectors, the effects will be focused and dramatic. A couple of examples illustrate the point.

The anthrax scare prompted the U.S. government to order millions of pills at a cost of 95 cents each, thereby injecting millions of dollars into the pharmaceutical industry. At the same time, a growing concern over the possibility of smallpox and other diseases created new opportunities for this industry to sell millions of doses that had not been projected in sales for 2001 or 2002. In fact, the problem they had was how to increase production beyond normal levels.

Securing telecommunications infrastructures became an overnight opportunity for computer services firms around the world. The IT industry, which was having a lackluster year in 2001, suddenly found that companies and government agencies wanted to beef up the security of their networks and information processing systems. Quickly, it looked like demand was reaching gold rush proportions, but without much publicity, because no organization wanted its customers and stockholders to know that some vital systems perhaps were anything but perfectly secure. Just as pharmaceutical firms had to find new ways to make more doses faster, firms providing high-tech services faced a parallel challenge to protect the nation's information infrastructure.

There was a precedent involving penicillin during World War II after American health officials concluded that it was an effective treatment for infections, a problem faced by wounded soldiers and civilians. In 1943, only a few thousand doses could be manufactured. Pharmaceutical firms were then put under enormous pressure to find a faster way to make more. By the end of the war, they had succeeded, producing tens of thousands of doses. To do that, they had to fundamentally change production processes. As a result, after the war, these firms could keep up with the worldwide demand for this miracle drug.

We would argue that the American experience is on the side of optimism in the face of tough times and crises. But positive results can take time. In the 1930s and early 1940s, it took time and a war to solve the unemployment crisis after the heroic attempts by the Roosevelt administration to end the Great Depression initially failed. World War II changed everything within a year of America's entry into the conflict. The demand for soldiers, government employees, and workers to manufacture goods, grow food, and perform services essentially created a zero unemployment situation. The demand for labor propelled millions of women into the workplace, filling jobs that historically had been held only by men—in manufacturing, auto repair, construction, and munitions plants. Wars do that by stimulating military and secondary demands that expand the work force, often in ways new to the economy. What woman in 1939 would ever have thought that, in a few years, she would be building B-17s? Or assembling machine guns?

Manufacturing was transformed. During the 1930s, the IBM manufacturing plant in Poughkeepsie, New York, made accounting equipment. During World War II, it made rifles and handguns with *IBM* emblazoned on their barrels. NCR manufactured Norden bomb sights that made it possible for B-17s to drop payloads on enemy cities from high altitudes. Examples of transformation spread throughout an economy adjusting to new realities, as happened in one way or another during the Civil War, World War I, and the Korean and Vietnam Wars. The IBM example personifies what happened.

Thomas J. Watson, the head of the company and an unabashed patriot, assured the American government that his firm would make all its services, assets, and people available for the war effort. Of course, he also knew these services would be paid for but, that point aside, what counts is the results. When Watson's executives and government officials in the War Department looked at what IBM was good at, both concluded that this company had precision machining skills, knew how to mass-produce complex metal products, and had fully staffed factories already in place. With that set of capabilities, it was not a huge reach to conclude that instead of making metal parts for accounting equipment, IBM could make metal parts for rifles and handguns. And just as the company knew how to put little metal parts together to make business machines, it could also put little metal components together to make weapons. The same kind of transformation from civilian to military goods took place across the economy, as is occurring today.

Specific changes that constitute improvements also spring up, as with cockpit doors. For years, safety experts had been trying to get U.S. airlines to replace their lightweight, flimsy cockpit doors with secure, bulletproof ones, like those the Israelis insist their airlines use. American firms balked at the cost of the doors and the additional fuel consumption to carry the extra weight. Companies selling the doors just could not make a sale. Then came 9-11, and essentially, the American public said, "We won't fly with you until you fix your doors." U.S. airlines got the message and immediately began refurbishing most of their fleets with new doors.

THE CHANGING NATURE OF WORK

The nature of work itself was already undergoing significant transformation over the past several decades as a
backdrop for the impact of the new normalcy. The ways in
which it is already influencing these trends are likely har-
bingers of what will emerge. Historically, three long-term
trends stand out.

The first has been the shift from traditional manufacturing jobs to what economists call *service sector* jobs. Much
more than waiters, cab drivers, and hamburger flippers are
included. Add doctors, lawyers, engineers, architects, consultants, and senior executives. Even in most manufacturing companies today, the percentage of people who
physically make things is often less than 10 percent of the
employment rolls; in high-tech companies, it is often less
than 5 percent. So the number of people who hammer,
bend metal, and assemble has been shrinking as a percentage of the total work force, while service sector jobs requir-
ing technical skills have been increasing.

These service sector jobs involve a second economic
trend, the rapid increase in the reliance on computing as an
integral part of how work is done. PCs, telecommunications, and now the Internet represent the most visible and
obvious examples of where work is headed. Today, over 65
percent of all workers use computers in one fashion or
another, up from less than 40 percent 15 years ago. A less

obvious (and related) trend has been the ongoing shift of work responsibilities to robots and computers in general. The shift began with robotic devices that paint cars and with drafting systems that design parts of products by performing the necessary calculations and making decisions regarding them. Next, computers conducted transactions, such as automated telephone conversations. Other systems automatically decide where to reroute trains, control movement of natural gas through pipelines, and adjust manufacturing processes in response to changing conditions. This shift to computers in getting work done and making decisions has occurred across numerous industries in both the service and manufacturing sectors.

The third major trend is the shift of technologically sophisticated work to employees in the U.S. and of less skilled work to other countries. The change in who does what and in what countries also has led to a more mobile work force. People in the service sector and highly skilled workers can and do move from company to company more quickly and more easily than ever before. The flip side is that, as work moves overseas, companies hire and fire more readily, as circumstances dictate.

In wartime, every nation wants to locate within its borders all the capabilities it needs to avoid depending on others for critical supplies. In the 1980s, some American leaders worried when Japanese computer chip manufacturers increased their world market share at the expense of

American suppliers. They feared that if the U.S. went to war, the Pentagon would have to rely on the Japanese to provide components for advanced weapons systems. However, the market turned around in the 1990s, as U.S. suppliers introduced a whole new generation of computer chip technology. U.S. chip manufacturers now make the most advanced products, while the Japanese and other overseas producers make less sophisticated chips. The age-old concern about having all the necessary capabilities remains, raising serious questions: Does the United States have all the assets it needs to support a war effort? Will it have to rely on allies for critical support, some of whom may waver over time in their backing of a war effort?

Nonetheless, while there are no guarantees in any war, particularly a global, decentralized struggle against terrorism, the U.S. is in a strong position. It makes more food than it consumes and has one of the best trained, technologically equipped work forces in the world. Add its formidable size (over 100 million). During the 1990s, the nation's businesses strengthened themselves by trimming fat and waste in many industries and by upgrading technologies. So we entered the war against terrorism in better economic shape than in any other war, with the possible exception of the Vietnam War (which began after the nation had just experienced over 15 years of outstanding economic and technological advancements). In contrast, at the start of World War II, an observer could have stressed the negatives in worn-out factories and a work force scattered due to unemployment. Still, the country was able to modernize, organize, and out-produce all other nations in the war. Rather than making a jingoist statement, we are pointing out that the country and its economy have latent vitality, which economists and social planners can fail to factor into an assessment of the outlook.

Despite fear and uncertainty, this state of the economy supports confidence and determination (but certainly not complacence). There are signs everywhere that the economy can do what needs to be done at the rate and volume required. At the same time, we also have the ability to invent or innovate new production and work processes to meet the demands of new circumstances. The combination of the two makes it possible to capitalize on new economic opportunities and to change existing procedures and types of work.

Overall, the nature of work is changing, and its future is already arriving to the point where we can stop, look, and identify what's happening. The directions are manifest. Individually, they signal change. Viewed holistically, they amount to a nationwide environment that is like the air we breathe or the water in which fish swim. It is taken for granted, always there, hardly visible from one Monday to the next. In times of crisis and change, we need to take notice of what is happening.

First, work is becoming increasingly technical. Computers are standard tools of any and all trades. Computers and other technologies will be used to automate and to perform ever more complex tasks. This entrenched process will speed up because war economies have an urgency that peacetime economies do not.

Second, there will be more jobs in those industries that directly support military activities: food production, weapons manufacturing, transportation, medical supplies, telecommunications—everything the Pentagon needs to wage war and government agencies need to protect the homeland. At first, it is business as usual in the way things are done, but soon, processes, operations, and even organizations morph as circumstances dictate. Out of such transformations, new types of work appear and, thus, new job opportunities. Such opportunities replace jobs that go away.

Third, it is quite possible that economic globalization may slow down as the physical movement of merchandise and service sector people declines in the face of potential dangers and shifting demands. If that happens, existing regional trade arrangements become more significant, such as more trading within the boundaries of NAFTA or the European Common Market and less from one trading region to another. The one major exception, and it could be an enormous one, is trade resulting from the military needs of allies. If, for example, Lockheed makes a military aircraft that is adopted as the standard by armed services in Europe, then its planes will be traded within the Common Market. Since aircraft now cost millions of dollars and in some cases approach a billion dollars per airplane, the amounts of money involved are enormous.

Meanwhile, lesser areas of trade could suffer. The overheated 1990s banana trade problems between the U.S. and Europe can be seen as a harbinger of problems for other products in the global economy. Slowdowns can hurt industries dealing in luxury items, such as jewelry and exotic foods, books, paintings, clothing, especially those from the Middle East. Trade will slow down in products deemed of significance to national security, such as medicines (e.g., smallpox vaccinations), advanced computer systems (which the U.S. blocked from being sold to the Soviets during the Cold War), and raw materials needed to support military and civilian defense needs. These include fuels of all kinds, ores of all types (e.g., iron, zinc, copper), and possibly even foods (in our case, grains and cattle). It echoes what happened during World War II.

Fourth, national assets used for the development of new knowledge and products, such as universities, government research laboratories, and company R&D facilities, would have their work agendas shaped more by government priorities than by economic opportunities. This trend would create new jobs and at least change the focus of work for some people, as they develop new materials, foods, medicines, and technologies. For others, it will mean operating in larger organizations as the appropriate setting for large tasks with high national priorities.

This shift in work and priorities takes place in two established ways. The U.S. government, through existing agencies, the most important of which is the National Science Foundation, already funds a high proportion of basic research in the United States. Just by shifting its funding priorities, the government can prompt research organizations to change theirs in order to win grants. Government purchases are a second powerful influence upon the workplace and marketplace. The federal government remains the single largest customer in the U.S. economy and has been since the end of the 1920s. Such was also the case in every war, with the exceptions of the Spanish-American War of 1898 and all wars and conflicts prior to 1845. Within the U.S. government, the largest single buyer is the Pentagon. Put another way, the American government uses up 18 to 19 percent of the national GDP in peacetime, a percentage that increases in wartime.

Fifth, as individuals, we should be prepared to pursue multiple careers, rather than one lifelong career. This process began in the 1960s as the economy shifted increasingly from manufacturing to services and as whole new industries came into being (such as software). By the 1990s, the outlook for the "average American worker" was changing dramatically to employment at several companies during his or her lifetime and pursuit of two or three fundamentally different careers. New workplace demands, opportunities, and circumstances all drive the process by which new careers and jobs emerge and old ones go away. While it is difficult to forecast the specifics, it is not difficult to recognize the reality. Accordingly, changing our mindset to match this reality can be viewed either as an opportunity or a calamity. Given what historian David S. Landes told us about historical processes, opting for the optimistic view puts us in a position to be on the winning side of jobs, careers, and history.

DECENTRALIZATION OF WORK

In all probability, the disasters of 9-11 will speed up the process of decentralizing work that is already widespread throughout industrial societies. The process was well underway before the Internet made mobile work possible for all types of service and white-collar jobs. In reflecting on the fact that thousands of people work in high-rise structures around the world, we think of what happened on September 11 in the World Trade Center and ask, Does this still make sense?

The traditional arguments in favor of centralization are familiar. Concentration of employees optimizes the use of scarce land in downtown cities and makes it possible for people to communicate and collaborate efficiently. It brings prestige to a city and symbolizes a nation's prosperity. But as we saw with 9-11, the destruction of a towering office building can wipe out 50 or even 75 percent of a company's employees in a centralized operation. In the aftermath, many New York financial organizations announced that in finding replacement office space, they were going to scatter their employees across multiple buildings. Neighboring New Jersey was an immediate beneficiary after 9-11, gaining 15,400 jobs in October alone.

The shifting of work from one state to another and from one country to another is pronounced in the American economy. The creation of NAFTA accelerated the process as high-tech work clustered in the U.S., while low-paying, unskilled work tended to migrate toward Mexico. The process is global as, for example, in the shift of computer chip manufacturing to Asia. Today, in a reflection of decentralization, no industry in the "advanced economies" builds factories with 30,000 or more employees. The economics of factory building and management suggest that a more optimal size is normally under 10,000, which means that, as economies and industries expand, there are more factories and offices scattered around the world.

For Americans, there are economic incentives to decentralize work forces as fewer companies concentrate thousands of employees in one location or high percentages in tall buildings or even in sections of a major city. Companies and government agencies have good reason to do so and not only for security. Decentralization enables companies to stay in closer touch with the customers and communities they serve. Thanks to the information infrastructure, decentralization works smoothly, as telecommunications and computer technology carry the process further, making telecommuting feasible. In the U.S. alone, over half the homes are connected to the Internet; over 90 percent have telephones. High-speed telecommunications exist in every community in America, eliminating distance as a management problem.

The process has been spreading for several decades, even though, historically, industries tended to develop in one geographic location for the convenience of suppliers and employees. Automobile manufacturing, for example, was once concentrated in Detroit; now, factories are scattered across the nation. Tennessee has become a major auto producer. New York City, historically the center of clothing manufacturing, has been joined by foreign manufacturers. Well over one-third of all clothing in America is imported from as far away as China and Israel. As the banking industry rapidly consolidates into huge enterprises, made possible by telecommunications and computing, headquarter facilities are dispersed. Online banking, in particular, is available across the nation; branch offices are widely scattered. ATMs provide access to accounts of multiple banks through a single machine that accesses banking networks.

Families can live and work just about anywhere, whether they earn their income in service or manufacturing, as the U.S. population disperses throughout all 50 states and urban centers expand faster than the population. We now have cities, such as Austin and Phoenix, with more than several million residents that, even 20 years ago, were far from qualifying as urban centers. This trend, actually underway since the late 1800s, has so far shown no indication of slowing down. Good highways, extensive air transportation, and far-reaching communications, along with an ample supply of workers (often new ones in the form of immigrants), have made this historic trend possible. The resources have been there to make it possible—the nation's supply of clean water and the ability to produce more than enough food to feed itself.

The new normalcy is bound to stimulate the dispersal of work across the nation for security reasons alone. Since the process is already underway for sound economic reasons, it is likely to accelerate in those industries that have remained too concentrated, such as the financial sector in New York. The U.S. government will probably follow suit, in keeping with the dispersal evident in the 1970s and 1980s, as members of Congress use their influence to shift federal facilities and activities out of Washington, D.C. into their districts for political reasons.

The new normalcy has already meant more physical security in public and commercial buildings as the war on terrorism expands security efforts. Actually, security concerns are not new. Unnoticed by the public, corporations have long been concerned about the kinds of security issues that Americans are now hearing about. For decades, large companies have been the subject of attacks, scattered and targeted, but nonetheless real and frightening to those directly affected. An incident in a Midwest city, another in South America, a third in East Asia become grim reminders of the need for vigilance. Multinational corporations have received the message and have developed company-wide strategies for protecting themselves.

From kindergarten to college campus, from factory to research laboratories, from government buildings to branch offices, America no longer takes security for granted. Strangers can't enter buildings without showing badges, getting passes, or being escorted. In the 1990s, quietly and without fanfare, concrete barriers went up at entrances to offices and factories to prevent terrorists or disgruntled employees from smashing vehicles into these buildings. There is hardly a major office or factory in the country that does not have little cameras mounted on corners, in lobbies, and over entrance ways that feed continuous video images to a security office. Companies began installing these in the 1980s. Corporate and government employees receive several communications each year with guidelines on how to protect information, keep secrets, and secure laptops and other assets. An eerie reminder for everyone was the U.S. Post Office advisory on protecting ourselves from anthrax.

At city, state, and federal levels, government has assumed an increasingly proactive role in maintaining security. Where lapses or breakdowns occur, response is immediate. Measures have been taken to use digital and other technologies to improve tracking of movement into and out of the country. Within weeks of 9-11, Congress provided extensive surveillance powers to law enforcement agencies. While such powers make some Americans uncomfortable for constitutional reasons, survey after survey finds the public willing to tolerate this as part of the new normalcy. Similar powers and practices, which have long existed in other liberal democracies in Western Europe, Israel, Japan, and Australia, have proved to be effective. Clearly, what counts with a security-minded public is taking actions that work.

For decentralized workers, who rely on telecommunications and travel, this means less privacy and more tracking of their movements. It is a relatively new experience for Americans but mainly of degree. For decades, there has been a steady buildup of accessibility to personal information about finances, spending, travel, and debt. The failure of government agencies to share information in an organized way reflected America's aversion to a society in which "Big Brother is watching." The breakdown in sharing was evident in the aftermath of 9-11, when it turned out that government agencies were not exchanging the wide-ranging information about the movements and activities of suspected terrorists. Increased surveillance and coordination require adjustments as computer and telecommunications technology facilitates the integration of information, although more slowly than law enforcement officials would like. The task is not easy.

As industries and the American work force decentralize, information about people, data, and activities is centralizing. As the process broadens, we can expect renewed discussions about personal freedom, privacy, and constitutional protection, because the new normalcy will bring these issues to our attention. If history is a guide, there will be some extreme intrusions, which the courts will knock down, while additional monitoring of personal activities and information becomes a part of the new normalcy. Security comes at a price. The adjustments will transform and expand the federal government's role in the way Americans work, in the taxes they pay, and in how funds are used.

THE NEW ROLE OF GOVERNMENT

The new normalcy has already enlarged the role of the federal government in ways that would have been inconceivable before 9-11. Normally, we think of government expanding during Democratic administrations and shrinking under Republican control. In fact, all during the 1990s, while President Clinton and the Democrats ran the government, public expenditures and employment at the federal level declined. During the Bush administration, the reverse occurred after 9-11, despite Republican aversion to federal spending and an expanded federal role. Security needs alone forced the national government into playing a more active role: more military, more criminal investigations, greater airport security, more investigations of bioterrorism. The list keeps growing.

A similar pattern emerged at state and local levels. The first signs appeared when overtime costs ballooned spending for police and fire protection, followed by the need to add staff to handle security. When and if security problems worsen and wartime needs expand, we can expect government agencies at all levels to grow and spend more across the entire economy, forcing a shift in resources from the private to the public sector.

Another trend centers on government's role as shaper of the nation's priorities and leader of the public's responses to crisis. In times of uncertainty, we invariably increase our trust in and reliance on public officials. We look to them for direction, what the press and commentators call *leadership*. One reason Mayor Rudy Giuliani became so popular nationally (even internationally) in the weeks following 9-11 was the way he came across as a leader. The nation saw him repeatedly on television at the scene of the 9-11 disaster and heard him repeatedly reassuring the country and providing guidance on how to respond. During the Great Depression, President Roosevelt became a popular leader for doing the same thing. His signature statement became "The only thing we have to fear is fear itself." During World War II, he gave the nation direction: "We must be the great arsenal of democracy." During uncertain times, guidance and leadership become a major function of top government officials, constituting a major national asset in times of crisis.

In pointing the way, leadership animates the country and lets everyone know what to focus on and why, thereby leveraging the assets of the economy and the support of the public. It is a hallmark of democratic government in mobilizing its citizens. In any democracy, the role of government leaders is clear: to persuade the public to embrace specific programs by tapping the fundamental values of the nation. Roosevelt's overriding message in World War II spoke to the basic American belief that the nation had a historic mission to foster democracy and freedom around the world. Americans heard and answered the call.

In addition to becoming more involved in security and playing a heightened leadership role, governments expand their control of economic activities in uncertain times. Essentially, four activities take on greater significance.

The first is economic policies that reside in programs introduced or expanded to stimulate specific objectives: creation of new jobs, control of inflation, encouragement or discouragement of foreign trade, and manufacture of goods needed to defend the nation.

The second involves tax policy. This is not limited to collecting more taxes to pay for larger and better equipped military forces, although this is clearly important and necessary. Tax policies allow governments to reinforce economic objectives, such as stimulating the creation of new jobs and encouraging the public to spend or save more. The U.S. government has long recognized the powerful influence of tax policies on institutional and personal economic behavior, a sensitive feature of any capitalist system. While economists have long argued that the effects of U.S. tax policies take more than a half year to actually kick in, the American public reacts immediately by changing its economic behavior to take advantage of anticipated changes. As the new normalcy takes hold, we can expect changes in tax laws to have more dramatic effects than in peaceful times. In 2001 alone, that already happened.

Third, the federal government spends more money. In every war and even in periods of recession and depression, doing so "buys" the nation out of problems. The highly influential British economist, John Maynard Keynes, argued in the 1920s and 1930s that modern economies could best be managed by a more proactive government role in economic affairs. This involves managing classic market forces, even in free enterprise economies, to deal with recessions and depressions and to provide safety nets for those in need.

The Roosevelt administration in the 1930s adopted Keynesian economics hook, line, and sinker, as has every administration since then. President Lyndon B. Johnson funded both the Vietnam War and his Great Society programs simultaneously by driving up the national debt. President Ronald Reagan did essentially the same thing as he sought to outbid the Soviets in an arms buildup. U.S. governments have not hesitated to spend in times of crisis, and the national economy has normally been strong enough over a long enough period of time to handle the increased debt. Such is the case today, and we can expect more of the same in facing up to the new normalcy, although it means taking money out of the economy that consumers might spend on cars, appliances, redecorating, and luxuries.

Fourth, money is used as a weapon. This tactic, used in times of both peace and war, is called *foreign aid*, one of the most misunderstood uses of money. It is designed to do basically two things: reward some nation to do something the U.S. wants done or as an economic incentive to have another nation work with the United States. A current example of the first use is the construction of roads financed by the U.S. so that military vehicles can move around in an underdeveloped country. An example of the second is the post-9-11 aid to Pakistan to encourage its participation in the fight against the Taliban. A variation of both objectives is aid for political and moral reasons, such as food to an area hit with a natural disaster.

Foreign aid is administered in a variety of ways. Most Americans think it is handed over to governments as cash and checks to spend as they wish. That is not normally the case. Usually, money is earmarked for specific projects, often managed by international agencies or with a variety of audit controls in place. Another way is to provide credit to be spent within the U.S.—for example, to purchase weapons made by American firms, but not for military items manufactured by a third country. The same applies to grants for medical supplies and earth moving equipment. This has the double effect of providing a grant for political reasons while creating jobs and pumping money into the U.S. economy. Normally, foreign aid represents a tiny portion of the U.S. government's budget—less than 1.5 percent—even in generous times, but it gets more negative publicity than just about any other public expenditure. Yet, it remains an effective and popular tool used by government in uncertain times. Understanding how foreign aid is expended gives companies and individual entrepreneurs valuable insights into opportunities for new sales to other countries. It is also part of understanding how the recent past shapes and influences policies and practices in dealing with change.

NEW OPPORTUNITIES AND LOST CAUSES

There is a saying Ecuadorian Indians use to describe life that fits the current situation: "When you put your hand in the river, you forever change its flow." We cannot reverse what has happened. We have to respond and react. Our hand is in the river. As change begets more change, nothing remains fixed, and the water flows differently. That means old practices will disappear, and new circumstances will make new demands and deliver new opportunities.

Rather than guess which businesses and enterprises will win or lose over the long run, clearly an unrealistic exercise when things are changing so quickly and so unpredictably, a review of key influences on winning and losing in the short term is more promising. We can look first at how people respond to increased restrictions on freedom of movement and threats to their security. As air travel becomes more time-consuming because of security checks, alternative forms of transportation become more attractive, such as train service between New York and Washington. If we were travel agents, we would think about becoming experts on rail and bus travel. We would look for travel arrangements that provide a secure environment. We would look for solutions that speed up and streamline how things are done in the new (not the old) normalcy. We would do so in a society where "time is money" and where the business culture rewards cycle-time improvements.

With regard to security, the issue is less about selling more guns and gas masks, although many businesses are doing that, and more about spotting clues to new directions in needs and wants. In the weeks after 9-11, for example, real estate agents and bed and breakfast owners reported a sharp increase in activity as people from large cities either sought a refuge from urban centers (which seem to be targets) or looked for short vacations that did not require flying. Does this portend a new flight to rural and small town America? Does this suggest more vacations by car within the U.S.? Does this foreshadow an increase in job searches in the U.S. heartland? How much do we factor in the maturity of the Internet and the enormous shift in how work can be done online? Clearly, jobs and careers can be dispersed across the nation in ways unimaginable a decade ago. Ingenuity-driven opportunity knocks for telecommunications, computing, real estate, the battered entertainment and travel industries, and home furnishings. Demographic shifts will be inevitable as a by-product of concern about security and the cost of living in expensive cities, not to mention the aging of the U.S. population.

Meanwhile, manufacturing firms and large service enterprises that respond to the newly expanding needs of U.S. government agencies will find manifold opportunities driven by war and homeland security programs. The question, How can we serve the market? quickly became a hot issue for businesses. As unemployment increases, government programs are likely to subsidize job-producing activities and offer opportunities to hire more people without the full burden of salaries. Linking hiring initiatives to defense and security considerations holds further promise of economic activity.

What doesn't represent an opportunity? The short answer is anything that runs contrary to what is happening in the economy and to what the public needs and wants. As public confidence about job security declines, major acquisitions, such as cars, appliances, and furniture, will be put off as much as possible. Even home purchases are vulnerable to a decline, despite mortgage costs that have not been so low since the early 1960s. Why? People do not want to be saddled with increased debt in uncertain times. As to government exhortations to shop in order to stimulate the economy, they run up against the fear factor. Americans who are afraid of losing their jobs are not going to run out and buy a new car.

Among U.S. companies, fear of declining revenues and shrinking profits demonstrated its chilling effect even before 9-11. Firms in many industries reduced capital expenditures and much of their discretionary spending for consulting, meetings, training, and travel. As with the American public, unnecessary expenditures were being cut back with a nervous eye on the bottom line.

In pursuing opportunities to sell goods and services, an economic pullback suggests that the prospects for small expenditures are better bets than for large ones. Redecorating a kitchen may be out, but not new curtains. Buying a new car may be postponed, but not necessarily a DVD player. A trip to Paris may be out, but not one to Montreal. Even usually impregnable wealthy Americans are backing off conspicuous consumption as the nation's mood shifts from self-indulgence and excess toward prudence and moderation. This does not mean that people will stop going out to dinner and on vacation, but they will go out less often and to less expensive places, and will look to economize on their vacations. At home, they are more likely to cut the lawn, rake the leaves, and shovel the snow themselves. It is up to opportunity seekers to look around and take advantage of the trends and changing attitudes in society as careful replaces carefree.

We can expect increased demand for solution-seeking among both companies and individuals. In uncertain times, individual Americans focus not on overnight wealth from dot-com IPOs, but on guidance in how to conserve what they have and in how to spend less. One example is the surge in refinancing mortgages—which has kept bank officers busy. Or the tendency to repair the family car, rather than trade it in for a new one, meaning more business for car mechanics. Terrorism, with its ruthless reminders of mortality, prompts people to put their affairs in order— which leads to appointments with insurance brokers to write policies and with lawyers to write wills. The equivalent in company life is the pursuit of economies (limiting travel, limo rentals, hiring, purchasing, and bonuses) and the search for sound, long-term decisions on a range of crucial business issues—expansion, cutbacks, layoffs, mergers, business partnerships—all of which demand a range of services from accounting and law to consulting and outplacement.

Successful craftspeople apply a strategy of flexibility in their respective fields of business. For instance, iron workers who know how to put up steel staircases in buildings learn to install aluminum balcony rails, then to do ornamental brass work for a hotel lobby. It is all work with metal, but with a difference that involves getting in sync with the marketplace. If buildings are not being put up, then remodeling lobbies can replace putting in staircases. For some, work flexibility can involve additional training, an advanced degree, or a change of career (drawing on skills, aptitudes, and interests). It can mean transferring what we have to offer from one industry or type of organization to another, such as an accountant interested in classical music changing from administering salaries and benefits in a manufacturing plant to become a financial officer for a symphony orchestra. A public school teacher becomes a trainer for a consulting firm, an editor of a trade magazine becomes a Web site editor, a medical doctor becomes an executive at a pharmaceutical firm. Similar skills and/or interests, different venues.

By focusing on our strengths, we can identify our role in society and find a place where we can make a contribution. Self-awareness draws on an old American value, self-reliance. It counters a sense of vulnerability with a strong dose of personal responsibility in taking charge of our individual destinies. Essentially, Benjamin Franklin was referring in 1757 to this American value in the quaint language of the eighteenth century when he stated, "He that hath a trade hath an estate and he that hath a calling hath an office of profit and honor."

Flexibility, adaptability, and a sense of responsibility constitute an optimistic response to the major changes of the past 20 years in the American economy. The changes surround us: the effects of the Internet on business organization and practices; the increased turnover in jobs and careers that the "average" person is experiencing; the changing skills required to perform desirable jobs; and the rising requirements for undergraduate, graduate, and other forms of credentialing just to rate an interview, much less to keep a job or to get promoted. When jobs turn over, as in the recession of 2001 and especially after 9-11, a form of musical chairs gets played out in the workplace. Just as in the children's game, if you do not find a seat, you are out of the game and must watch while the others keep playing. At a party, that means being left out of the fun; in real life, it is a financial disaster and a personal crisis.

As we argue throughout this book, churn has been increasing. 9-11 probably has heightened the tempo and certainly increased awareness of change at every level of American life. That is why it makes sense to take stock of what we are good at and leverage our skills by holding jobs that play to those strengths or by seeking employment that does. In the final analysis, finding our way at work is a solo flight in the sunset of a secure bygone era of one lifetime career, one company, one job. More than ever, individual men and women are on their own in a competitive global environment, just as companies are.

It is appropriate to borrow the concept of core compe-tence and apply it to ourselves as individuals. What we know and can do is what counts. Experience on its own has become an increasingly unreliable asset. We can no longer feel that longevity guarantees security for the individual or survival for a company. Just as breakthroughs, takeovers, and new technologies can endanger companies blocked by inertia, so can new methods, techniques, products, and ser-vices endanger jobs and professions that are taken for granted. The subtext of change can become obsolescence and displacement. Or it can translate into new opportunities. If we cannot continue to thrive by manufacturing cash registers (in wartime) or motorcycles (in peacetime), we need to identify and act on what we can do to meet the needs and wants of a rapidly changing marketplace in a global, decentralized environment. Fortunately, as we will discuss in the next chapter, America has the human, physical, economic, and technological resources to respond to the challenges we face—a portfolio of reasons to support optimism.

5

LEVERAGING AMERICA'S RESOURCES

We are given one life and the decision is ours whether to wait for circumstances to make up our mind, or whether to act and, in acting, to live.

OMAR BRADLEY, U.S. GENERAL, WORLD WAR II

B eyond the front pages of American newspapers, with their attention-getting headlines, and past the exhortations of their editorial pages, we find evidence and examples of what the nation is all about. We read obituaries that mark the passing of men and women who lived 80 to 90-plus years, each a witness to the strengths of America and an embodiment of the human resources our nation can draw upon. In chronicling the lives of pillars of local communities, obituaries celebrate the forces that hold the country together.

In reading obituaries, we find a reassuring pattern of life in our country. Typically, a long-lived male will have worked in the same profession or industry for 30 to 40 years and will have belonged to the same religious denomination for his entire life. While women will probably accentuate their role as mothers and grandmothers, even great-grandmothers, they follow a similar pattern, particularly with affiliations in churches, organizations, and charitable groups, covering a variety of roles: alumnus, job holder, parent, war veteran, club member. If the deceased had been a businessman, we may read about a Rotary Club membership or a long-standing association with the local Chamber of Commerce. These affiliations have the ongoing effect of binding Americans together as fellow members interact with each other at local, regional, and national meetings, events, and conventions. Americans as "belongers" create a style of behavior, a set of consolidated values, and a network of activities and associations that help to define the individual and his or her identity. As a pronounced American characteristic, the pattern of joining suits a nation of immigrants. It is a standard American way for newcomers to develop a sense of belonging.

In accentuating the positive, obituaries celebrate what means the most to Americans by affirming the national trinity of God, Home, and Country. Obituaries honor "solid citizens" who participated in community life while working hard and raising families. When called, they responded by helping out and joining up. Tribal, engaged, optimistic Americans who live into their 80s and 90s have much to teach us. They are men and women who experienced the Great Depression, World War II, Korea, and their children's protests of the 1960s and 1970s. They set or maintained trends discussed throughout this book. They are reminders that change breeds opportunities and that optimism has long-term staying power. As for us, we are *they*, on the way to being *them*.

In an overall appraisal of our strengths, Americans in all their variety constitute the nation's rich human resource. Individual initiatives, support, and participation—coupled with the contributions of organizations, companies, and the national government—shape our ability to confront crisis and to meet the challenge of change. We are living in a country where variety is a source of strength and our strengths a reason for variety, thereby attracting the best and brightest from all over the world.

A NATION OF JOINERS

For all our variety, we are interconnected, intersected, and interwoven by organizations—arguably more so than any other modern nation. Organizations are deeply rooted in cities of all sizes, a tradition reaching back to the frontier building of the nation, when neighbors had to rely on neighbors. Every community has nonprofit charities to help the poor and needy, commonly organized into coalitions, such as United Way. Disaster relief organizations exist throughout America, from full-time to volunteer fire departments to emergency response teams to volunteer medical services. The Red Cross is 100 percent an American original. Every community has associations that support development of local economies and quality of life. They are distinctively American institutions: Chamber of Commerce, Rotary, Kiwanis, Lions, women's clubs, garden clubs, sports clubs. From the Aaron Burr Association to the American Society of Zoologists, the endless list of organizations offers something for every conceivable joiner. Drive into any town or city in America, and the first thing you are likely to see is a sign with the little round emblems of the service organizations that have chapters there.

Invariably, industries, crafts, and professions have their organizations, ranging from the American Medical Association to the American Historical Association to unions for truck drivers, manufacturing employees, electricians, and actors. These are typically organized into local chapters, which then integrate into regional, state, and finally, national organizations. Every community has a collection of churches with regular memberships and attendance that expand in difficult times. Churches, in turn, organize into community-wide coordinating groups as interfaith councils with an accent on cooperation. Starting with Cub Scouts through Boy Scouts, Brownie Scouts through Girl Scouts, and Little League baseball, the call to join up starts young and continues through the varieties of senior citizen groups. Over the years, Americans accumulate memberships in a variety of organizations, each connecting us in one way or another—by what we believe, do for a living, enjoy doing, take an interest in, or want to do to help others, our communities, our country, our world.

Even passive affiliations create memberships. Graduating from college, for example, automatically makes us members of an alumni association and recipients of announcements, alumni magazines, and fund-raising solicitations for the rest of our lives. The result is a nationwide army of alumni in a country with nearly 2,000 colleges and universities in America and a population in which about 25 percent of all adults have been through some form of higher education. Another major source of passive associations is the support we shower on local sports teams, most of which maintain fan support organizations. These associations can be as active (and vocal) as any special interest group. Avid loyalties link strangers as fellow fans in arenas and bars in cheering for home teams, particularly in baseball, basketball, hockey, and football, women's teams included. Depending on the team, fans even develop group characteristics—from long-suffering Chicago and Boston baseball diehards to usually triumphant Yankee fans.

The dual characteristic of American organizations—rooted in their communities yet also linked regionally and nationally—is a major (easily overlooked) source of national unity and strength. Within organizations, their branches are in contact with each other continuously and, as the occasion arises, with other organizations. These contacts draw on a 200-year history of coordination and response. As a result, when a crisis occurs, as in New York, well-organized, trained resources respond immediately to help.

The important point to make about organizations in America is that they are always there, actively serving the community. They address economic, social, political, and religious ends. Local citizenry are routinely energized and mobilized to solve problems and meet community needs, from saving historic sites to setting up neighborhood watches. Typically, the Chamber of Commerce helps the local economy by recruiting new businesses to set up shop. Each fall, United Way fund-raising campaigns are as American as Fourth of July parades. Church-based charity drives, particularly for food and clothing, are regular features of almost every community in America. The custom of delivering Thanksgiving meals to the needy is as American as the turkey on the table.

Governments follow suit in casting a wide net to involve the citizenry. Regional planning commissions are an example. Members appointed to quasi-public or official boards by mayors and governors deal with everything from cultural affairs to running a military draft board to planning economic development. They are natural extensions of the American penchant for joining organizations and for involving citizen volunteers.

Organizations channel and energize the desire to make a difference by establishing what is tantamount to a standby infrastructure that combines know-how and professionalism. Organizations add meaning and significance to the deep-rooted American desire to make a difference. By structuring that desire, organizations sustain the impulse to volunteer beyond a crisis here, a problem there, making it possible for the Red Cross to collect blood all year long, for United Way agencies to help children and young adults 12 months a year, and for local fire departments to train and be prepared for small and major disasters. The volunteerism rooted in the American frontier is being updated once again within the context of the new normalcy. The motivation itself is essentially unchanged. We Americans want to come together to protect ourselves, to create economic opportunity, and to improve quality of life, all in our community's best interests.

When Americans contribute their time, money, energy, and know-how to organizations, they draw on their entrenched tradition and habit of volunteerism. It is a major national asset that we should not overlook. Not all necessary and vital activity in this nation is performed by paid employees or government officials carrying out their responsibilities. In the late 1990s, a national survey found that 56 percent of Americans over 18 volunteered 19.9 billion hours in one year, a total estimated at 109 million participants in 1998. Seventy percent of all households contributed to charities. When asked, eight of ten Americans donate. America's volunteer workplace has been estimated as the equivalent of over nine million full-time employees and valued at $225 billion. Small wonder at the outpouring of donations, time, and effort in response to 9-11.

Volunteerism is so intrinsic to American life that it is almost impossible to conceive of the United States without organizations that serve a wide range of needs and interests. There is an important practical side to this phenomenon. It means that we can (and do) mobilize quickly to help individuals, ourselves, our communities, and our country. It is a silver bullet that can and should be leveraged in various ways.

It makes sense for Americans—who have a range of concerns and interests—to seek out more than one organization from the long list of possibilities. A single organization is unlikely to cover all of an individual's priorities; too many are likely to spread us too thinly. Once we join up, we are able to meet on a regular basis to discuss our concerns, find outlets for our energies, and, most important, become involved. Through organizations, individuals can do a great deal to calm fears, share information, and identify ways and means of benefiting the community. For the individual, participation is psychologically gratifying and fulfilling. A feeling of helpfulness replaces a feeling of helplessness. Channeling our energies as a volunteer and drawing on the available options make it possible to work on what we think is important, relevant, and, indeed, critical during uncertain times. The result is a win-win situation for the individual, the community, the country.

When Americans decide on where to join up, their interests essentially fall into three areas: economic, communal, and religious. On the economic front, it is all about building a local economy in which the largest number of those who want to work have a job, and the others are not abandoned. The community front involves a wide range of needs, from physical security and protection of life and property to the upkeep and enhancement of the physical setting. The religious need involves participation in a church, synagogue, or other formal religious organization. The infrastructure for involvement exists in every community, a way to increase control over our own lives and to reduce the anxiety caused by uncertain times.

It's up to government at all levels to take advantage of the human resources out there, ready and willing to help. To a degree, this runs counter to the government tendency in the second half of the twentieth century to want to do all its own work and, at best, share only a limited amount of it with outside groups and individuals. Volunteer organizations in states and communities can be leveraged to help secure the nation, improve services, and enhance the country's sense of well-being. Mayors, governors, and federal cabinet officials should ask themselves how volunteer organizations can help the nation at local, state, and national levels. How, for example, can they help protect transportation, find jobs for the displaced, identify strategies to improve information security, protect civil liberties, feed the hungry, recruit military personnel? How can churches and United Way agencies improve literacy, enhance education, and reduce government's need to focus on welfare, while it concentrates more on national defense?

We cannot assume that organizations by themselves will accidentally or intentionally answer these questions in ways satisfactory to public officials, who should take the initiative in identifying what volunteers can do, provide channels for helping, and asking for that help. In turn, organizations should turn to their local and national leaders and ask the same question, How can we help? The spirit of such cooperation and collaboration is grounded in President John F. Kennedy's 1961 Inaugural Address: "Ask not what your country can do for you—ask what you can do for your country."

A national human resource that should be leveraged is retired Americans. We are talking about a pool of experienced, knowledgeable, and motivated people in the tens of millions. They include Americans who retired in their 50s and 60s, in excellent health and mentally alert in their 70s and 80s, even 90s, They are a growing population, most of whom are either already on pensions or working part time, so they are not a burden on the economy. We need to find ways to marshal that human reservoir to help do the nation's work. Many are already organized as members of the American Association for Retired Persons (AARP), church-related organizations, and nonprofit groups, but many also are not and need to be recruited. They come from every industry, every profession, and every faith. They can teach, do office work, provide skills and expertise. Many are veterans of the armed forces and, thus, have a heightened sense of patriotism that motivates them to help.

By beginning with national leadership and government agencies, then including nonprofit organizations, older Americans can and should be called upon to become active members of the many organizations that already exist or to expand the amount of time they spend helping their communities. Often, it boils down simply to asking for their help, then finding meaningful tasks for them to do. It is a sad state of affairs that society's veneration of youth has marginalized so many older Americans. In the new normalcy, we need to follow the practice of other societies in keeping our senior citizens engaged in the mainstream of the nation's life. If government does not take the lead, why not the AARP, which already has national community service programs? A stepped-up effort could bring about formation of a nationwide response that surpasses that of the Peace Corps.

Ultimately, being a volunteer provides satisfaction for Americans of all ages, whether it is school children taking up collections or seniors doing financial audits. It is also thoroughly American in a society whose citizens have long understood the Biblical call to charity. In First Corinthians (13:13), we are told, "And now abideth faith, hope, and charity; these three; but the greatest of these is charity." It is not only a charity of food and money donated, but also of time and leadership given. At Harvard University, in the entrance to its inner campus, Harvard Yard, a basic philosophy for today's Americans is reaffirmed in stone: "Depart to serve better thy country and mankind." In that universal formula lies personal fulfillment and the feeling that, rather than being helpless, individual Americans can take part in controlling their lives. In that way, personal fulfillment has practical benefits in uncertain times.

NATIONAL SECURITY AND HOMELAND DEFENSE

For America, the challenge of terrorism is less military action abroad and more defense at home. It's a new experience for Americans, one that involves everyone for the unnerving reason that it threatens everyone.

In any assessment of the challenge, the military part is not a major concern. As in the past, the U.S. military performs at a level that satisfies and reassures the American public and government officials. At budget time, defense expenditures do become an issue, and at various points, discussions about one technology initiative or another arouse fierce debate (and intense lobbying). But, as the situation stands, the U.S. military community is working better than ever before in a coordinated manner across all the services. Military personnel are well trained and, for the most part, do have the military technologies they need. They also have the abiding affection and support of the American public, and when crises arise, people volunteer to serve, as happened after 9-11.

Withal, there are still issues to resolve. Convincing arguments are made for increasing the number of permanent in-uniform personnel over the next several years. Calling civilian reservists into active duty to reassure air travelers is reassuring but not a permanent solution. Neither is assigning reservists to handle the myriad assignments the military has around the world. While the expense of additional military forces is high, so are the dangers great, as laid out by our national leaders.

In this regard, the United States has a historic pattern to deal with. The government ramps up its military establishment in times of war and even more quickly demobilizes when peace returns. At the end of the Civil War, World Wars

I and II, and again after both Korea and Vietnam, we reduced the size of our standing uniform services, slashed their budgets, and basically made it difficult for the military to be prepared for emergencies and crises. To be fair, the Pentagon did not help itself with sloppy, even wasteful, accounting and purchasing practices. Congress adds to the problem by pushing programs primarily because they benefit home districts, by promoting the manufacture of equipment the Pentagon does not need, and by keeping unnecessary bases open.

In the face of a global buildup of military hardware and power, the world has become too dangerous a place to run a military establishment on a rubber-band principle of fast expansion and even faster contraction. It is not enough just to rely on smart bombs and high-tech bombers to do the job. The generals make a powerful case that America needs more of everything—more men and women in uniform, more pilots, and more equipment—in both peacetime and war. To use boardroom terminology, the volume of business we have today—and will probably have for many years to come—calls for more of everything the military uses and needs, even if it means tolerating some unproductive practices on the part of many government agencies. It is, as a tried-and-true slogan reminds us, "the price of freedom."

In contrast with military preparedness, homeland defense has emerged as a new nationwide challenge for Americans. On this issue, the administration got it right. It recognized quickly the need to coordinate internal defense and transcend normal police work, with a quasi-military dimension added. Then came the enormous problems of creating an effective homeland defense, which requires a combination of strong public support and government leadership. The problems are legal and bureaucratic, practical and political, managerial and intellectual.

LEGAL RAMIFCATIONS

The passage of legislation to try terrorists by military courts represents the public and governmental determination to protect the nation and its people. At the same time, there are safeguards for civil liberties to ensure the rights of American citizens, along with provisions to treat foreign nationals within the context of international laws and treaty obligations. A reversion to a nineteenth-century practice is underway, whereby the U.S. Army handles certain domestic policing actions that it was not allowed to do internally in the twentieth century. There is enough precedent from the past to indicate that this can work out when military and nonmilitary legal and police elements share the same respect for civil liberties and avoid turf battles over jurisdiction. Still, using military courts is not without controversy. Both civil libertarians and political conservatives are extremely nervous about this new authority. Fortunately, there is general agreement that it should be used carefully and wisely—in other words, infrequently and with all due care.

Agency Turf Battles

A major reason for creating a homeland defense administration was to coordinate and leverage the capabilities of various U.S. government agencies in the campaign for intelligence about terrorist activities. Throughout most of the twentieth century, the FBI focused on internal criminal issues, while the CIA spent its half-century of existence focused on external threats. From Day One of the new homeland initiative, there were turf battles, and concerns about what legal mandates to follow while overcoming lack of recent experience in coordination. Now various agencies must share data and coordinate their efforts. While they did that in the past, particularly during the Cold War, it was done selectively, usually in very limited ways and under restrictions of national law and prior legal practices. Now they need computer systems that talk to each other, and their representatives have to work as teams, meeting and sharing information and coordinating activities.

The IRS has to work with the Departments of Commerce and State, while agencies across all departments communicate with each other for the first time. It is a major shift in how government works, and many public officials are uncomfortable about how best to do this. In addition, law enforcement agencies from county sheriff departments to the FBI will have to share information, despite the reluctance expressed by some officials in the past. Federal agencies, in particular, will need to be encouraged and, if necessary, compelled by law to work closely with each other and with local government.

MANAGING BUREAUCRATIC RIVALRIES

Every large corporation has a basic problem: Each division or line of business (LOB) tries to act independently of other lines and sometimes at cross purposes. LOBs compete for attention, resources, and credit for results. Cross-LOB rivalries remain the chronic scourge of all large organizations, including the U.S. government. The rivalry at a Navy-Army football game, while legendary and good-natured, is an annual display of a deep-seated problem within the U.S. government, an enterprise that employs over one million civilians, in addition to another million-plus military. Experienced senior managers will admit that rivalries hang on, despite the noblest intentions of all involved. Top management can minimize it here and there, in certain ways and for limited periods of time, but rivalries in the federal government are as enduring as the Washington Monument.

Former Pennsylvania governor Tom Ridge, as director of the Office of Homeland Defense, faced the problem much like a general without an army. Provided with few laws to provide legal authority for imposing cooperation, he was handed the task of getting agencies that normally do not work together to do so, ranging from the military to park rangers, to state governments, to county sheriffs, to each individual American. He ventured forth without resources, staffing, or organization, all of which required Congressional action to establish a cabinet-level department set up in close sync with well-established government agencies, including the FBI, Secret Service, parts of IRS, and the CIA. Agencies within the Departments of Commerce, State, Labor, and Interior also have a place in such a setup.

The situation presents an opportunity to learn and apply lessons from business and to make organizational changes within the U.S. government. When companies find they are organized for purposes that are no longer relevant, two scenarios come into play. First, those in organizations rapidly losing effectiveness try desperately to hold on, to find relevance, and to resist change. Second, senior management forces through reorganizations that align the organization with its current mission. Governments do this, too, but far more slowly and less frequently. Practices that are well understood within corporations reduce rivalries and, more important, improve effectiveness. An appropriate target within the federal government is the range of law enforcement agencies, from tobacco and firearms enforcement to protection of the president. In fact, the Secret Service is in the Treasury Department. We have the FBI, as well. Within the intelligence-gathering community, the Pentagon has the National Security Agency and, of course, the CIA. They all claim to have specialized missions, but the reality is that their missions overlap, as is evident in how they perform their daily tasks. The situation cries out for streamlining and integration and the terrorist threat to America is a compelling reason to do this now. It will save money, expedite sharing of information, enhance coordination of investigations, and facilitate preventive actions.

In the area of economic development, we have the Departments of Labor, Commerce, and Agriculture, in addition to miscellaneous agencies scattered throughout the government. Leaving aside the political constituencies that exist in support of various interest groups, do we need a Department of Agriculture in a nation where farming makes up only 5 percent of the GDP and probably about 1.5 percent of the work force? We need food, but can't that department become an agency in a reorganized Department of Economic Development? Such a department could integrate Commerce and Labor and coordinate economic development, notably by stimulating development of products that reduce our dependence on oil. Even the Department of State—the agency that is supposed to handle all of our international relations—can use a makeover. For one thing, there are many agencies in other departments involved in foreign affairs, such as the Department of Commerce in promoting trade. What happened to the role of consul generals in the State Department? That used to be one of their top two or three missions.

GETTING IT ALL TOGETHER

A two-step plan of reform is called for. The first step involves giving Tom Ridge the staff and legal authority to integrate the sharing of resources and information to address immediate problems. Second, start the process of fundamentally redesigning the organization of the federal government. This has been done several times in American history, although never as efficiently as routinely occurs in business. But it can be done. The last time this occurred was during the Roosevelt administration of the 1930s, which had to respond to the terrible conditions created by the Great Depression. Earlier in U.S. history, other reforms begun at the start of the Civil War of the 1860s continued for an additional two decades, as the nation expanded in size and entered the Industrial Age. Even earlier, from the 1780s until the end of the War of 1812, substantial changes came about: creation of two constitutions, passage of 12 amendments to the second constitution, and creation of whole new departments (War, State, Treasury) and agencies (such as the U.S. Post Office). The government is not bound to keep today's departments and agencies in perpetuity when closing them down and creating new ones will produce far better results. Politicians and lobbyists will roll their eyes, but ultimately, the government will make changes if the voters clamor for them. So we must clamor and advocate.

While the first step needs to be done quickly and even ruthlessly, the second one should be done incrementally and thoughtfully over a period of years. The changes needed for Tom Ridge to fulfill his mandate should take place in one year or so. Second-stage changes probably need at least a decade. Given the war on terrorism, law enforcement is an obvious first choice, followed by economic development. The Pentagon, despite all the stories we read about waste and inefficiencies, has a history of incrementally changing things internally, despite enormous resistance by the uniformed services. The support for change already exists. Before 9-11, the hot issue at the Defense Department was what should be the mission of the Pentagon over the next decade. Secretary of Defense Donald Rumsfeld was advocating many changes, while many senior officers in the uniformed services were resisting. He seemed to be slowly getting his way until 9-11 put that all aside for the time being. The transformation on the near horizon in the Defense Department needs to spread across the entire federal government.

What about state and local governments? Should they change, too? The answer is probably yes. But with so many variations in the structure and work of these governmental entities, any generalizations are on shaky ground. But three issues do stand out for state governments:

- As the federal government transforms, look for opportunities to align or complement changes in operations within the states.

- As the need for better coordination and efficiency in law enforcement increases, find ways to improve coordination among all agencies, from federal to community level. This may require changes in criminal law.

- As states begin to show readiness to cooperate regionally, look beyond environmental issues to regional industrial development and common tax systems, so that neighboring states don't compete with each other for businesses.

COMPROMISES IN CIVIL LIBERTIES

To make the homeland initiative effective, its leadership asked for and received additional authority to do wiretaps; conduct searches of homes, offices, databases, and PC files; and arrest and detain people for extended periods of time. Americans have always been of two minds on this issue. On one hand, they understand and accept the notion that, for a period of time, traditional civil liberties might have to be compromised for the good of all. On the other hand, they realize that public officials can go too far in the zeal to do their work and need to be reined in. Getting that balance right has never been easy, as circumstances shift and situations change and as we judge people on an individual basis. All must be in sync with our bedrock constitutional principles that people have undeniable rights and are assumed innocent until proven guilty. These values make particular demands as the nation pursues security in a search for suspects of Arabic background, while respecting individual rights.

In the overall reaction to 9-11, leaders in what was characterized as the Arabic community have been criticized for condemning the terrorism belatedly and, thereby, fomenting suspicion of all Arab Americans. The criticism reflects the risks in stereotyping. Third- and fourth-generation Americans of Middle Eastern descent are as assimilated as any other descendants of Ellis Island, heirs of a migration in which 90 percent of Arabic-speaking immigrants arriving before 1924 were Christians. Coming from Greater Syria, which included what became Lebanon, they typically made a point of separating themselves from Arabic Muslims.

This same Muslim-Christian antagonism led to the insanely bloody 1970–1985 Lebanese civil war. Here in the U.S., only in recent decades have Muslim Arabs begun arriving in significant numbers, as in Detroit and in New York City's borough of Brooklyn. They have swelled a Muslim community in the United States that is not only Arabic. It includes a number of Africans and Asians, a mixed group that lacks a strong network of organizations and strong leadership. This helps to explain the failure to immediately denounce Arab-based terrorism, a failure which ill-served the Arab American community.

At our physical borders to the north and south, we have come face to face with the before-and-after of 9-11. Those who travel frequently understand how open American borders have been, starting with the U.S.-Canadian border which had minimal controls over who goes back and forth. The Ambassador Bridge between Detroit and Windsor, Ontario was the world's busiest land-border crossing, by which 5,000 trucks entered the U.S. every day. There has been long-standing pride in the openness of that border, a mark of deep friendship and mutual respect among the people of both nations. But the door could not be kept wide open after 9-11. At the Ambassador Bridge, five inspectors were taking three hours to fully check out a loaded 18-wheel truck. The result was massive delays, part of tightening border procedures, tracking travelers, and watching for suspected terrorists.

On the Mexican border, by contrast, security has been a long-standing issue, going back half a century. While recent organizational changes in the mission and role of the U.S. Immigration and Naturalization Service will help, the U.S. government must work closely with Mexican officials to implement the consequences of NAFTA. That means more work permits for people coming and going in tracking border movement. Mexico, for its part, needs to increase the effectiveness of its internal security operations, working far more closely with American and European police agencies, so that Mexico does not become a point of entry for terrorists. Ensuing changes could essentially merge the economies of Mexico and the United States, fulfilling the ultimate vision of NAFTA. That would be a positive by-product of uncertain times because of the well-documented performance of Mexicans who have come to the U.S.

Mexicans, like other Hispanics, come into the U.S. as some of the poorest newcomers, then move the fastest into the middle class. Once employed, they have one of the lowest unemployment records in the nation and the highest two-jobs-per-worker rate. Their work ethic would make any New England pilgrim proud. They have great entrepreneurial instincts and readily form new businesses, then expand them. Other Hispanics display the same characteristics, sharing the deep-seated values of family and country that hold sway in the United States. They are religious and invest extensively in education for their children, whom they make the centers of their family lives. They have a propensity to join the armed forces and then serve with distinction. Patriotism, personal commitment, and physical ability make them good soldiers, sailors, and pilots. As the fastest growing minority in the U.S., Hispanics constitute some 11 percent of the total population, solid citizens and hard workers.

The Hispanic experience in the United States and contribution to the nation constitute a current chapter in the country's historic role as the refuge of "huddled masses yearning to breathe free" (as inscribed on the pedestal of the Statue of Liberty). President Franklin D. Roosevelt, whose family came over on the Mayflower, added a celebrated reminder to the DAR: "Remember, remember always that all of us, and you and I especially, are descended from immigrants and revolutionists."

For immigrants, the United States remains the land of opportunity, as well as freedom. For the United States, immigration has been and remains a source of talent, energy, skill, brainpower and national strength—in human resources. Pointing this out raises the stakes in a war on terrorism, when a land of opportunity confronts suicidal fanatics out to destroy what a nation of immigrants created by capitalizing on freedom. And, for harsh symbolism, their infamous deed on 9-11 was in full sight of the Statue of Liberty.

National outrage, which is warranted, must lead to a national strategy, which is necessary as we keep freedom alive, side by side with self-defense. There's no escaping the thorny, complex issue of civil liberties when a democracy is under attack. What should government and individuals do? Prior wars suggest a useful strategy and four basic actions that involve Americans as a people under siege.

First, government agencies need to track the activities of suspected terrorists more closely (economic transactions, political statements, illegal activities), while applying a modicum of increased legal authority to interrupt an individual's activities and to penetrate privacy. Such intrusions must be warranted as direct and provable support of national security. The good news is that the United States has taken action on this front that is practical and effective.

Second, collection of information about people's activities should be coordinated and systematized, something that we have started to do already, with laws that have made credit checks and reviews of criminal records possible online. Government agencies can employ the same practices used by marketing departments in major U.S. corporations. Instead of *know thy customers, know thy citizens*.

Third, if you enter this country, you should be held to the reason you're here. If you have a visa to go to school and you don't, you should be expelled. If you are on a work permit or tourist visa and you stay longer than allowed under the terms of that visa, you should be put on a flight out of the country. There is nothing unusual about such policies and practices in most countries around the world.

Fourth, citizens and civil libertarian organizations should be on the alert for assaults upon civil liberties. We must keep pressure on the government to stay within tolerable and acceptable bounds, pressure Congress, and institute lawsuits (wherever necessary) to preserve the delicate balance between the government's need of oversight and the constitutional rights of individual citizens. This strategy, which is difficult to implement, requires constant attention and can feel elusive, but nonetheless, it has demonstrated its workability throughout U.S. history. It comes down to the historic tension between the fundamental rights of democratic freedom and the need for personal security.

WHAT TO DO ABOUT TERRORISTS

In developing an overall blueprint for combating terrorists, we can learn from the U.S. war against drug dealers in Colombia. To deal with the immediate problem of containing the drug lords, the U.S. trained and supplied the Colombian military, which hunted down and arrested or killed drug lords and their associates. This discourages others from working with them. While buying time and producing some positive results, it is not a complete solution. The underlying economic, social, and political problems remain. Ultimately, that means providing economic incentives for farmers to grow something other than cocaine, creating a middle class, and protecting civil liberties and property rights.

The Middle East, source of anti-U.S. terrorism, presents a similar scenario. Military initiatives to hunt down and kill or arrest terrorists and those who support them (people, organizations, even nations) will provide immediate results and are necessary. But the sources of the problem are endemic and structural and, therefore, demand more than quick fixes from the outside. Doing something that endures is difficult and will take time and tough decisions.

Looming over the Middle East, with its history of colonialism, dictatorships, and unstable governments is the Israeli-Palestinian conflict and its impact on U.S.-Arab relations. The American government faces an on-again, off-again choice of brokering a deal satisfactory to both sides or of standing aside and letting the two sides struggle until one wins. The first approach, a mixture of hope and frustration, has alternated between expectation and disappointment. The second is political anathema because of America's long-standing support and commitment, bulwarked by the influence of the Jewish vote. What everyone wants to avoid is an explosion of war that can come about if Arab governments topple and extremists take over. Too often, the decisive vote in Middle Eastern politics (both in Israel and the Arab countries) can be the assassin's bullet.

Second, we face the problem of our oil dependence. Every American administration and the U.S. public have long known the solution: End that dependence. We must face the reality that there are insufficient supplies of readily available oil within the U.S. There are untapped fields in Alaska, which in all probability will be extracted over the protests of environmentalists, and other pools of oil in Canada, the Gulf of Mexico, and elsewhere in Latin America. As a coordinated response, the U.S. government can create economic incentives, work with the environmentalists, and cooperate with governments in the hemisphere to obtain more supplies of oil.

Meanwhile, American industry is gradually finding ways to optimize the operations of machinery to reduce the need for electricity and oil. In the case of automobiles, the long process of improving gas mileage and adopting semi-electric vehicles has started—slowly. As a nation, we need to speed up such trends with the objective of reducing U.S. consumption of Arab oil to less than 25 percent of our total needs within a few years. In that way, less dependence on Middle East oil can mean more independence and flexibility in U.S. foreign policy, although abandonment of Israel is inconceivable, given the political, diplomatic, tactical, and moral factors in play.

Third, we have the problem of poverty and the huge gap between rich and poor in the Middle East, a problem that the U.S. cannot solve. In the past, when U.S. administrations have encouraged Arab states to adopt economic modernization programs, the results have been mixed. The U.S. has also encouraged Arab countries to open up their political processes and introduce democratic reforms. However, when that was done, radical right-wing parties—representing the poor of a nation—usually did well at the polls, bringing to power regimes hostile to the United States. Repeatedly, U.S. policy makers had no choice but to support friendly authoritarian regimes which kept radicals more or less in check at a cost of little or no democratic government. As long as nations in the Middle East are burdened with poverty, lack a middle class, and fail to modernize their economies, promoting democracy is risky business. That is a tough pill for Americans to swallow, but historical experience supports the observation. Meanwhile, by working with other nations, international organizations, and the well-educated, and by maintaining relations with authoritarian or conservative rulers of many Arab nations, the U.S. can continue to promote the creation of modern economies and a middle class. People who are making car and house payments are less likely to throw bombs.

Building a middle class in poor regions of the world is possible. It is happening across large tracts of East Asia, in the expanding middle class in India amidst a nation with great poverty, and in Mexico. It is a process still in motion, one in which the poor live alongside the rich and the middle class, and eventually move up economically. That is the good news; the bad news is that this process takes more than a generation to implement. In China, for example, senior leaders expect it to take up most of the twenty-first century.

We are left with the fundamental problem of deciding where to throw our support. While aligning ourselves in the past with authoritarian regimes has often provided short-term benefits, it probably has been costly in the long term. In those countries where the American government supported such regimes, as in Nasser's Egypt and King Faisal's Saudi Arabia, the U.S. did not win the hearts and minds of the populace. Where the U.S. criticized dictatorial regimes, as in Iran, there was public sympathy for the American cause after 9-11. As far as radical Muslims are concerned in any of these countries, they are in the minority. The key point is what Middle East experts have been pointing out for years: when America's foreign policy does not live up to America's values—democratic government, individuality, personal accountability, civil liberties, freedom of religion—we are seen as hypocrites by the Arab public. When the United States aligns itself with an authoritarian regime, it demonstrates hypocrisy, and, thereby, loses respect in the region.

U.S. leaders must choose. Do they continue to support authoritarian regimes in foreign policy or do they support American values? The choice is neither as obvious nor as easy as it appears. On moral grounds alone, we should support American values. If other factors must be considered, such as protecting access to oil, the answer becomes less automatic. It becomes more complicated if we pick and choose a democratic regime in one place and an autocratic one in another. Nonetheless, the faster we reduce our dependence on oil, the easier it will be to align U.S. foreign policy with American values, even in the face of the persisting Palestinian-Israeli conflict.

As Americans, we still do not need to abandon our sense of responsibility, particularly when terrorism presents an unequivocal target—suicidal fanatics whose agenda is death and destruction and whose indiscriminate target is innocent men, women, and children. It is not a problem limited to the Middle East. It rears its head in Asia, Africa, and South America. Wherever the threat arises, there is a policy to pursue that merits the support of Americans and is in keeping with our traditions:

- Crush terrorism around the world with direct military intervention or indirectly by supporting local military forces.
- Support economic development with a view to eliminating poverty, illiteracy, and disease.

The world is better organized than ever, with international organizations to mount such an effort. From the United Nations to the International Monetary Fund, the world is well served by the expertise and the experience of such organizations. The reaction to 9-11 has raised worldwide consciousness and created a climate of moral concern. There is a major change from the Cold War, when the U.S. often had to go it alone in its constructive initiatives, because it had the economic wherewithal and the political/

military need to do so. In the years to come, coalition building with organizations and nations will become an important part of American foreign affairs, building on early successes and lessons gained in the 1990s. This looms as a major opportunity to leverage the response to terrorism as the occasion for building a better world. Americans as individuals and the United States as a nation constitute a major resource in confronting the economic challenge to build a better world.

FORWARD ON THE ECONOMIC FRONT

I don't like money actually, but it quiets my nerves.

JOE LEWIS, 1948

Instead of turning to the proverbial cab driver for a reading on how Americans are doing in the face of economic uncertainty, we propose an upscale substitute more appropriate to an America after the euphoric 1990s. We nominate a suburban dentist with a thriving practice of patients representing an America of substantial mortgages, investments and debt, at least two family cars, sons and daughters at high-tuition colleges, and European (or at least Caribbean) vacations. They are discretionary spenders who fuel the U.S. economy.

Here's the dentist's report: "I don't know of a single patient of mine who doesn't have a family member or friend who has been laid off."

While military strategy and global politics command popular attention in times of crisis, the personal economic realities of jobs affect breadwinners and everyone else in their families, with ripple effects on everyone from local gardeners to restaurateurs, from hairdressers to Main Street jewelers. A familiar one-liner still gets it right: "When my neighbor loses his job, it's a recession; when I lose my job, it's a depression." When President George Bush lost his bid to win a second term as president in 1992, in the words of one commentator he lost because, "it was the economy stupid."

In the current crisis, a war against terrorism is complicated by prior economic strains on the national economy and on the individual American as job holder, taxpayer, and consumer. Employment figures for October, 2001, the first full month after 9-11, dramatized what was already happening. Employment fell by 600,000 jobs; unemployment rose to 5.7 percent. The recession became official at the end of November, confirming what any cab driver or dentist could confirm as far back as March of 2001 (the belatedly official starting point). Even for those who held onto their jobs, the "fear factor" was kicking in as colleagues, family members, and friends lost jobs. The fallout from 9-11 shook even both parties in the U.S. Congress into responding to the economic troubles that cast a dark cloud over the country and forced Americans to take stock of how they stand financially.

A PERSONAL ECONOMIC AGENDA

In uncertain times, the old farmer's strategy of "putting up" food for the winter suggests an approach for facing up to economic hard times. On one hand, we must step back and ask, Do I have enough of a cushion to weather an economic storm? Where and how should I cut back on spending? How secure is my job and my income? On the other hand, How should I take advantage of lower financing costs for houses and cars? What spending and which investments make sense? Am I taking good care of my assets?

Prudence dictates that we reduce our debts, rely less on credit cards and more on cash, and curb discretionary spending. That's in tune with a national shift toward a more somber, austere mood, which prompts Americans to reduce debts and pay down home mortgages. There's also a place for spending, as when we take advantage of zero percent financing to buy a new car. For many Americans, refinancing makes it possible to restructure their debts to save carrying costs. In other words, spend, but expend more wisely in case we lose our jobs or face lower incomes. The bigger our financial cushion, the more comfortable we can be.

Hiding our money in a mattress makes no sense. We must still shop and buy what we need to maintain our way of life. We still must invest money to make it work for us. As a nation, we depend on consumer buying and selling, which accounts for two-thirds of all economic activity. Just as voting calls for an informed citizenry at the polls, our economic system relies on consumers and investors who manage their spending and their money wisely and well. Based on what financial experts advise, there are universals to keep in mind:

- Set aside a percentage of income in tax-sheltered savings, such as a 401(k) or IRA, doing this regularly via payroll deductions.

- Invest in stocks and bonds, insofar as we can afford to do so. They deliver long-term financial power that benefits from the historic success of the most stable economy in the world. As our incomes increase, increase our investments.

- Buy a home as soon as we can swing it, especially after mortgage rates have hit a 40-year low. Those already with mortgages have refinanced either to lower monthly costs or to pay them off faster. Upgrading to bigger, more expensive houses is not recommended in order to avoid increasing our debt burden amidst uncertainty.

Long-term optimism supports this approach. As a strategy that combines prudence and initiative, it has met the test of time. As witnesses on behalf of optimism, the many new millionaires in America represent a tribute to the country as a land of opportunity. As individuals, we keep the economy moving as we go through life paying our bills, doing what needs doing, and providing for our old age and for the next generation. Americans in all parts of the country and in all types of communities (rural, small town, urban, metropolitan) have followed this thoroughly American lifetime strategy and over time have prospered. There is every reason to view the past and present of these Americans as a prologue to the future. Three assumptions about the future of America itself stand behind optimism for individual Americans and for their nation as a whole:

- The American economy will be robust and expand in the years to come.
- The personal standard of living and quality of life will remain high and probably continue to improve.
- Investors around the world will continue to find the U.S. economy the most attractive place to invest their money.

Our history as a nation supports confidence in the American economy as able to outperform any other in the world during the best and worst of times. This is the case, even though the U.S. economy is profoundly tied to that of other countries, with the negative consequences that go with it (such as U.S. recessionary fallout when Japanese banks get into trouble). America's ability to generate new economic activity and productivity enables the country to overcome bumps in the road. Recoveries are faster; people find new or different jobs more readily than in other nations, governments do not hesitate to practice Keynesian economics by spending to reinforce the social safety net and to get unemployed Americans back to work. Because the American economy stands out as dynamic, innovative, and technologically advanced, it has an edge in the global marketplace, further reason for optimism.

It is up to the more than 100 million working Americans to read the reports on what is happening in the economy. Like crews on sailing ships, they must watch for storms, monitor their routes, and check which way the wind is blowing. Within jobs and companies, we need to look for new opportunities and be ready to change course. Our horizons must extend beyond our current companies, even beyond the current industry we're in. We must be ready to go in new directions, particularly since life on the job no longer means the same company for life. (Eleven different jobs is the likely total in a lifetime of work.) Rather than read old maps to decide on where to set sail for, consider future-oriented questions that help us get our bearings and decide what to keep on doing and what to do differently.

1. Is demand holding up for our products and/or services? Is there a drop in revenues ominous enough to warrant a second look at business prospects? Should I consider making a change while I can still take the initiative to change jobs and/or companies?

Whether we work for a multinational company or own a local laundromat, our responses depend on our attitude, and our attitude depends on whether we are tuned into the marketplace. We need to think and act like opportunity seekers who are in the right place—a land of opportunities. America's economic history favors a proactive approach, from celebrated business decisions on a global scale to untold decisions in local enterprises. Stuart Crainer, who collected *The 75 Greatest Decisions Ever Made* (New York: AMACOM, 1999) lists forward-looking examples under such headings as industry inventors, supermodels, getting on, marketing magic, lucky foresight, leading by example, competitive advantages, bright ideas, and people power.

What counts is the viability of a decision. Will it pay off, whatever the enterprise—multinational company, celebrated brand name, or Mom-and-Pop store? A decision is called for, whether we own, run, or work for a business enterprise. We must make decisions or they will be made for us by the marketplace. While the business history of America is clouded by mistaken decisions that in retrospect could have been avoided, the landscape is brightened by celebrated decisions: Sears, Roebuck & Co. decision to add retail stores to its catalog business; Michael Dell's decision to sell PCs built to order direct to customers; Gillette's decision to focus on the high end of the razor market. They are the tip of an iceberg of decisions made by individual Americans. They are decisions to strike out on our own, to switch jobs, or to change careers to keep up with what's happening in the marketplace. As fluidity in the marketplace increases, each individual American becomes a company of one, managing a working life filled with key decisions on whether to go or stay, change or stay put, take a risk or stick to a familiar route.

Let's be clear on one point: We are not advocating that individuals quit their current jobs—far from it, since it does not make sense for most people, particularly during uncertain times. However, by taking a second look at our current job, we can identify ways to work better and, in the process, strengthen our position in the enterprise. As individuals, we need to take personal responsibility for supporting the success of the organizations in which we work. We cannot leave that responsibility solely to top management. In the process, people who have a sense of responsibility for the success of their organizations, no matter what their scope of influence, minimize the odds of being laid off while maximizing their career prospects. Even when airlines around the world laid off tens of thousands of employees in the aftermath of 9-11, they still kept tens of thousands of employees on their payrolls. Those who were let go had to identify and rely on their skills, know-how, and experience more than ever to keep a foothold in the workplace.

2. What do I know how to do that looks likely to be in greater demand within my company, my specialty/profession, my industry? Or somewhere else in the workplace? What should I do now to prepare to go in a new direction?

These questions call for answers at various levels. If we want to establish a new business or invest in one, we would look to new products and services that are needed, ranging from improving security to helping people deal with stress in a time of uncertainty. As religious activities increase, there is a need for more church-related goods. Flag makers, among producers of patriotic paraphernalia, experience an increase in demand. Private security agencies benefit, as do developers of software that can link existing sets of information. These obvious examples only hint at the range of possibilities in following an entrepreneur's rule: In a world where everything is connected, watch for the "ripple effect." That means searching out the effects of changes and events in all the nooks and crannies of the marketplace and society.

Doors open as well as close in changing times, and no one faces that combination of setback and opportunity more directly than the growing number of Americans displaced by recession and terrorism. Should we plan and expect to get rehired by our former company? Is the company still viable? Do we fit into its future plans? Or is it time to explore a new career? The latter question is tough to face up to, representing, as it does, a personal upheaval. But it's not far-fetched at all and can become a matter of facing the facts. One of this book's authors was trained as a historian with the goal of becoming a professor until he looked at the job market for history professors after completing his Ph.D. in 1973. The job market was a disaster, so bad that 400 to 700 hopefuls were applying for every opening. He looked at the situation and decided to look elsewhere. So he went about identifying which industry represented a growth opportunity in the years ahead. He concluded that it was computers, found an entry point into the industry, and has never looked back. Doors close; doors wait to be opened.

3. What should we consider doing, given specific trends and actions already in play in the economy at home and globally? How, in the first place, do we stay in touch with what's happening so that we face the future with our eyes wide open?

As with sailing a boat, pay particular attention to the way the wind is blowing in order to choose the best direction. Understand trends and watch for opportunities, a tradition that is deeply rooted in the American experience, as old as the Mayflower, as new as a successful IPO on its first day of trading. Business founders and owners are not the only entrepreneurs. The same enterprising mentality is shared by everyone who strives to do a better job than anyone else—from fellow employees across the hall to counterparts on the other side of the globe. To succeed in this highly competitive economy, we're all competing for our places in the ranks of productive men and women whom commentator Eric Sevareid has called the "lead players in the drama [of business]...The category of entrepreneur includes all the people who set out to change the corner of the business world in which they find themselves—yes—all the people, in a word, who push the system along its restless path." They do so with their eyes wide open, aware of social, political, technological, and economic trends. Why such a wide-angle lens? Because everything affects everything else in this global, interconnected world where a single software command can bring information, people, and processes together.

As to learning about economic and business developments and trends, arguably they are covered in America as well as—or even better than—Super Bowls and World Series. Particularly in the 1990s, coverage of business was transformed in a nation where stock market closings are read as avidly as box scores. Wall Street is on Main Street. From the *Wall Street Journal* to *Fortune*, business reporting and writing match or surpass in journalistic quality, range, depth, and readability the articles on the pages of *Sports Illustrated*. Add the booming business of business books, not only in number but in high quality. For good measure, continuous and knowledgeable TV and Internet coverage of business is always a click away.

Technology, which empowers terrorists as it transforms our society, must be understood if we are going to get a handle on what's happening in every area of American life. We do not have to be engineers to get a sense of how PCs and the Internet are changing our lives by reshaping the nature of work and opening up economic opportunities. Our knowledge is first-hand; we experience the changes personally. We need to add attentive consumption of newspapers, magazines, and television and to complement them with selective reading of the many books exploring the technology adventure. For example, a knowledgeable corps of fiction writers use clothes, science, technology, and society in the entertaining costumes of suspenseful plots. It is continuing education at its most enjoyable.

We need to factor in the political dimensions of our world. There's no escaping the impact. It matters at all levels of our lives how the American government is acting in society and in the world, what major political changes are underway in other nations, and how globalization is tying the world together. A newspaper, coupled with the daily habit of watching TV news and discussion programs, keeps us up on history as it is being made. Add newspaper editorialists and columnists to the mix, making sure to include the ones we disagree with. Continuously, books by influential figures introduce fresh concepts and add insights that help us make sense of the news we read, hear, and see in the daily stream of information. As a bonus, there is information-rich C-SPAN, which provides a first-hand look at official events and at influential men and women who shape events and/or write about them.

Over time, our consumption of information influences how we see the world around us, helps us figure out what we might have to do differently, and supports a sense of equilibrium amidst recurring shock waves of news bulletins and blaring headlines. If we just drift on the ocean of information and news, there is a clear and constant danger that we will feel bewildered, if not numb. The working alternative is to pick and choose our information sources with full awareness of their points of view and ours, too. That calls for a mixture of healthy skepticism and openness, neither accepting all information at face value nor prejudging every issue. More is required: looking for patterns and trends, courtesy of observers and commentators, as sifted and sorted by us.

What's our goal? It's the self-confidence that we have our bearings. We need to think through information to understand what is really happening, instead of what seems to be happening. It is no accident that many famous and successful people have praised this state of mind. Andrew Carnegie, the founder of U.S. Steel in the nineteenth century, argued that "immense power is acquired by assuring yourself in your secret reveries that you were born to control affairs." Joe Namath, the NFL football player who subsequently became a successful businessman, added an athlete's twist: "When you have confidence, you can have a lot of fun. And when you have fun, you can do amazing things." Eleanor Roosevelt said it best: "No one can make you feel small without your consent."

Confidence, coupled with knowledge, helps to get us through uncertain times at various levels and in our various roles on the job, at home, and in the polling booth. We live a lifetime of making decisions and choices, of spending and investing, of accepting and rejecting. We live in a country that supplies us with a bountiful supply of information to turn into knowledge and, thereby, empower ourselves. Alvin Toffler, the author of *Future Shock*, argues that "knowledge is the most democratic source of power." We think he got it right. It is not about being smarter than someone else, letting the government protect you, or letting your employer secure your future. It is about collecting knowledge and putting it into action in managing our lives and our careers. After all is said, we are in charge of ourselves in our free-enterprise economy and, thanks to the democratic version of capitalism in which we live, we have both a right and a responsibility to have a say in how the economy operates.

PRESERVING AND ENHANCING THE NATION'S ECONOMY

What should be done differently with the economy in facing the new normalcy? Should we let the Federal Reserve Board continue to control inflation and stimulate the supply of money for business to invest and for Americans to buy homes and cars? To deal with the high cost of the war on terrorism, should we increase national debt, in effect putting the war on a credit card? Or do we increase taxes, as the nation normally does in time of war? Of course, if our war on terrorism turns out to be relatively short, without presenting larger threats to the United States (such as Iraq), then the Federal Reserve can carry on its well-established role of monitoring the ups and downs of the economy. But if the new normalcy persists—and we think it will, regardless of whether or not the nation is deploying troops in combat—then there are broad issues to deal with.

A hallmark of healthy capitalist economies is the freedom to make and sell goods and to move them to market quickly and cost-effectively. As America tightens its borders, inspects the contents of trucks and airplanes, and otherwise tracks movement of freight, the physical movement of goods is bound to slow down and cost more, starting with new security procedures. Somebody has to pay the rising bill. For example, in the face of the changes in security pro-

cedures, airlines and airports announced that they would
have to find a way to surcharge customers several dollars
per ticket to cover these added expenses. Surcharges on
millions of plane tickets alone amount to billions of dollars
diverted from other expenditures—by both companies and
consumers. The entire economy will feel the effect in a
redirection of assets that is economically nonproductive,
but necessary.

Movement of people, as well as goods, is headed for
change. The trend toward telecommuting and work at
home is likely to accelerate as companies decentralize and
corporate headquarters shrink. Companies will feel the
pressure to rely on modes of work and collaboration that
reduce travel and face-to-face meetings. This would mean
more demand for software and technology that reduce—
even in large measure replace—traditional meetings: group-
ware that permits joint editing in computer-supported collaboration, software agents that can handle tasks such as
data searches and scheduling of meetings, teleconferencing,
desktop videoconferencing, meeting room videoconferencing, voice and written interfacing with the computer, white-
board technology/PC-linked projection screens.

Solutions are not obvious or easy to the challenge of
maintaining freedom of movement as not only a moral
right, but an economic necessity. Clearly, making sure
there are no bombs in trucks or planes is a priority, and the
American public already has accepted the inconveniences

that security measures call for. But we need also to look for new ways to speed up that process and drive down its costs. Luggage scanning is an early example of a technology that is being used more than ever. MRIs are no longer just for scanning patients to check for diseases. The technology can scan passengers, luggage, and cargoes. Demand for such technologies no doubt will provide an economic incentive for the manufacture of cheaper and better versions, which, in turn, will drive down the cost of security while speeding the flow of goods and people through the economy. In the process, it is likely that doctors will end up with better and less costly tools for medical diagnosis.

We would encourage the government to use its R&D budgets through the National Science Foundation and other granting organizations in combination with tax incentives to encourage further development of security-related technologies. America can draw on its well-established technical and intellectual capabilities to push forward development of passive technologies in support of security. In the short term, governments from the local through federal levels can stimulate demand for such tools by buying what exists, even if it means charging the public and raising taxes.

With regard to free trade, America has a long-standing record of supporting international organizations that are behind it as a matter of economic policy. The trend is so pervasive and has so much momentum that it is difficult to conceive of changing course as a result of the new normalcy. In fact, it should not. We should not freeze in our tracks on the issue of free trade because of terrorism and the war against it. The rationale for free trade holds up after 9-11, just as before. What can change is the mix of trade, as business improves for defense-related industries and temporarily shrinks for tourism, for example.

As government at all levels searches for additional funding to pay for the new normalcy and stepped-up security, there is a temptation to increase excise taxes. Such temptations should be avoided at all costs. Better to look for ways to sell and buy more goods to counteract any economic slowdown. The situation calls for on one hand a balancing act between the need to maintain security and prosecute the war on terrorism, and on the other hand the importance of maximizing the flow of money, goods, and services through the economy to ensure job levels and maintain the standard of living.

Promoting the development and expansion of industries that play to the strengths of the American economy is a strategy that has a long history of success. The semiconductor industry illustrates the point. America invented the computer chip in the late 1950s and dominated the world in its production from the 1960s through the mid-1980s. Then the Japanese began making major inroads into the industry in the early 1990s, raising fears that national security would be at risk because so many weapon systems and military aircraft would potentially rely on Japanese-made components. The actual outcome was a different matter. Over time, the chip became a variety of chips, from cheap memory units that make our clock radios work to very sophisticated, state-of-the-art technologies that could be used in supercomputers and advanced electronics. Over time, the Japanese, and later other Asian nations, focused on making cheap, low-tech chips, while America retained its leadership position in the design and manufacture of the most advanced chips.

The pattern has repeated itself in other industries as well, such as software, pharmaceuticals, and aerospace. In the case of chips, it was in the best interest of national security and the economy to dominate at the high end of the chip product line. It happened not so much because of specific government incentives but through the natural forces of the free enterprise economy at work in a world of growing free trade. Supporting such outcomes in as many industries as possible makes sense. That means avoiding overregulation, leaning toward deregulation, and helping the pattern along with tax and other economic incentives.

A variety of government actions—some complex, some simple—can help. For example, in the case of oil, give every American who buys an electric car a tax deduction in the year of purchase large enough to grow market demand for electric cars at double-digit rates. That probably means making the after-tax cost of an electric car 20 percent less than a new gasoline-powered car. Why 20 percent? Because you have to make the electric car cheaper than a second-hand gas guzzler. Maintaining that tax break over a period of seven years can turn around the domination of gas-fueled cars, thereby driving down the consumption of oil. The same formula can be applied to trucks and buses.

It's up to the government to create economic incentives for vehicle manufacturers not to jack up the price of electric cars, buses, and trucks by 20 percent to replace the revenue and profits lost when people stop buying internal combustion vehicles. Do the same for trucks. And while we are at it, let's figure out how to improve the performance of heating and air conditioning machinery by applying the lessons that both government and business have learned over the last three decades in improving gas mileage for cars. Much can also be learned about applying national policies from the Europeans, who have struggled with high fuel costs for decades. In our case, the issue is not high fuel costs. (We still pay less for gasoline than any other major nation in the world.) It is a matter of reducing our dependence on Arab oil while ensuring that there is enough energy to run the economy.

As demand for different types of vehicles, air conditioners, heaters, and so forth increases, it is inevitable that the industries producing them will develop new products and improve the technologies underpinning them. That is how American firms became global leaders in pharmaceuticals, computer technology, and telecommunications and why the Japanese became the champions of consumer electronics. A phenomenon that economists call *path dependence* was at work. Essentially, the idea is simple to explain, complicated to manage. As a nation acquires a particular skill and the resources to sustain it (e.g., raw materials, know-how, infrastructure), it builds on that body of knowledge and assets, rising to greater heights of productivity and economic success. That is what happened with the semiconductor industry. Every country has its examples: France with women's fashions, the British with Scotch whiskey, Germany with precision-engineered products, Japan with consumer electronics. Many countries can also share a common path dependence, although it varies somewhat from one nation to another. So while Korea and Japan have great skills in the design of computer chips, American firms have cutting-edge skills that give them a competitive advantage.

When governments focus national strengths and encourage applications in the marketplace, they leverage the power of path dependence. Economists single out the United States for its grasp of how this phenomenon helps to power the economy and for demonstrating how it works. In fact, America is a laboratory for learning about path dependence and its lessons warrant an even greater role in formulating economy policy on the community, state, and regional, as well as national levels.

Finally, while free trade is crucial to the country's future welfare, we must also aim at self-sufficiency in critical areas as we go forward. The nation already maintains that level in the most critical area of all—producing enough food to feed itself, an independence lacking in many developed and developing countries. We could shut down our borders, keep out food imports, get rid of free trade, and we would still have enough food and clean water to sustain the country for the foreseeable future. Protecting our food supply from terrorists and supporting U.S. agriculture during tough economic times deserves to remain the high priority that it has been for policy makers for decades. This is more than just providing farmers with subsidies or making sure our meat supply is properly inspected. It is also about ensuring that all the food groups are grown and made available across the economy at reasonable prices and protected from terrorists. The same strategy applies to the creation and distribution of electricity and access to the national highway system.

Food is also a tool of foreign policy, as demonstrated in Afghanistan. We dropped several million prepackaged meals into the country to help win the hearts and minds of the local population. The strategy makes sense. It has built good will in other countries in other times when there were natural disasters. Our variety of foodstuffs is so great that we can create and apply food strategies that are tailored to the distinctive tastes and preferences of a region and with respect to its religious practices. Bullets are not the only weapons of war.

WORK, BUSINESS, AND NATIONAL WEALTH

In a free-enterprise economy, people and companies continually find new sources of income and profit. In wartime, that is especially the case because of the economic stimulus from massive increases in military spending and in new government jobs. In some cases, the opportunities will get public applause, such as the manufacture of bulletproof doors for airplane cockpits. At the other extreme, there will always be unscrupulous opportunists, such as gas station operators who responded to 9-11 by jacking up prices at the pump while wholesale prices stayed put. They got what they deserved. State attorneys general went after them within hours, fining them within weeks, and calling on drivers to stop buying their gas in the face of "un-American" gas gouging. Historically, public reaction and business success have been on the side of responsible and ethical business enterprises that meet genuine needs created by new circumstances. The benefits extend throughout the economy, in line with the adage that "rising water lifts all boats."

Optimists can point to a historic pattern in which American business—typically with entrepreneurs in the lead—has identified potential demand for new products and services and put them on the market at the right time. When horse-drawn wagons and carriages were straining to provide needed transportation and, in the process, choking cities to death in unbelievable filth, along came the internal combustion engine and the age of automobiles and trucks. Earlier, when moving people and vast quantities of goods was necessary to the growth of the nation, the railroad made its appearance. New technologies have eclipsed earlier ones, met new needs, and exploited opportunities. This has been so much the case that, in hindsight, the timing seems almost magical. The latest example was the merger of telephony, TV-like technologies, and PCs in what today we call the *Internet*.

An infusion of serendipity and some "aha's" have helped in the emergence of new products and services, but the reality is far less glamorous. What happens fits the American gestalt: The new products and services are practical, they are responses to opportunities, and they appeal to a ready and responsive marketplace of customers. When economists analyze how this happens, they identify time-tested ways by which entrepreneurs, companies, and industries convert new technologies and scientific knowledge into profit-generating goods and services. Everyone can benefit from understanding how this plays out, since individuals, departments within companies, whole enterprises, and governments all can and do apply these techniques. Americans already use them at levels that surpass any other major country as another competitive path dependence that provides opportunities in the future.

One strategy involves academics who conduct research on basic scientific and technological issues and are continuously making new findings that can be converted into products. This is particularly the case with medicines, but has occurred in biology, engineering, and metallurgy in a long list of areas of opportunity. Typically, opportunity follows one of two directions. A university may file for patent protection, then seek out a company to bring the discovery to market and pay royalties to the school. Pharmaceutical and chemical companies have long practiced this strategy for leveraging new knowledge. With nearly 2,000 colleges and universities and with more scientists and engineers conducting research today in the U.S. than have ever walked the face of the Earth, we should see this process continuing at full speed. Since the federal government sponsors so much research through such agencies as the National Science Foundation and the National Institutes for Health, American know-how in channeling research to fill gaps in knowledge is bound to foster economic opportunity in the future.

A second strategy is the use of company laboratories to conduct applied research. The starting point is a search for practical applications based on scientific principles. The transistor—immediate predecessor of the computer chip— came out of research done at Bell Labs on the conductivity of various elements. Every major high-tech company does this kind of research, notably AT&T, IBM, GE, GM, pharmaceutical firms, and major software developers. Companies began employing this strategy just before World War I, and by the 1920s, even medium-sized firms found the case for such laboratories so compelling that, even in the heart of the Great Depression, there were hundreds of laboratories. Today, they are the source of most high-tech products in over 100 industries. We have created a research culture where scientists and engineers working in these laboratories are constantly trying to figure out how to convert today's findings into tomorrow's patent applications.

Once patented, products can be manufactured and protected or the rights can be leased out. IBM, for example, generates over a billion dollars in annual revenues by leasing out patents that it currently does not choose to convert into products or which can be applied in different ways. AT&T did this with its transistor in the early 1950s, licensing out the fruits of its research to over 250 firms that made things beneficial to the economy but that AT&T had no interest in producing, from transistor radios to hearing aids. Those spin-offs across the economy occur all the time, creating new opportunities for profits and jobs.

A third strategy for creating new products from scientific and engineering research leverages entrepreneurial skills with venture capital. This works in two ways. Venture capitalist firms look around for promising opportunities, drawing on know-how in evaluating both new ideas and start-up enterprises. The firms provide managerial expertise in converting a good idea into a profit-making enterprise. This can range from tinkering with left-hand scissors to converting a scientific principle for burning fuel more efficiently into a new automobile. Many of the dot-coms and software firms of the 1990s fell into this category. Typically, venture capitalists specialize in certain industries, such as software or medical equipment, drawing on expertise in identifying promising opportunities and bringing them to market. American venture capitalists are world champions at doing this. The entrepreneurial spirit of American business, coupled with large supplies of capital over the past half-century, have made it possible for investors to hone their skills. Alongside failures, there are so many success stories (and billionaires) that this has become a unique feature of the American economy.

A variation of this strategy involves well-established firms, such as pharmaceutical, chemical, software, and computer technology companies. They keep an eye on the periphery of their industries to see what new enterprises are coming into play with venture funding. Due diligence has already been done by a venture capitalist firm which has the know-how and experience. An established firm can then draw on its strengths after buying out an emerging enterprise: know-how in cost-effective manufacturing (thanks to economies of scale), capacity to integrate acquired products into existing product lines, and positioning to tap an established base of customers.

Many companies use all three strategies to ensure a continuous flow of competitive products and services to offer their customers. While these practices exist in other countries, they flourish most in the United States, increasingly in parts of Western Europe and in some East Asian economies. The strategies have been so pervasive across so many industries for such a long time in the United States that many top managements take for granted this opportunity-seeking. It has become a natural part of what they do. However, we would argue that awareness of these practices and attention to the variables involved would improve the chances for success in pursuing ventures and increasing company yield. On their part, top managements and public officials can encourage companies to be more proactive, particularly in industries where innovation is already quite high (e.g., software, medical equipment, medications) or needs to be stimulated (e.g., steel, construction materials, and building practices).

All three strategies enable individuals to apply their knowledge and either build successful careers within universities and companies or create their own enterprises, as did Bill Gates with Microsoft and Andrew S. Grove with Intel. Companies can profit by adding products with high profit margins, as is the case with IBM, Dow, and other major companies. The strategies make it possible to optimize the use of investment dollars in wealth-creating opportunities, as was evident in the 1990s with high-flying IPOs. For federal agencies, these practices provide channels for influencing the nation's research agenda, while providing subsidies to higher education in exchange for practical results.

In these uncertain times, we can be certain that individual entrepreneurs and companies will look for new wealth-creating opportunities, and many will be successful. The nation will benefit in exchange, just as it has over the past 150 years, as the process of building companies with new products and services became ingrained in the business of America. Along come new jobs as a by-product. To be sure, old jobs disappear. You can no longer find anyone who hand paints automobiles in a Ford or GM factory, but you do find skilled workers who maintain and repair the robots that do a better job of painting cars than do people. The moral of the difference is found in every major forecast of new job creations published by the U.S. government over the past three decades. The forecasts emphasize the need for more workers in areas of emerging technologies—more medical professionals, software developers, engineers. As predicted in "a survey of the near future" by Peter F. Drucker, "knowledge technologists are likely to become the dominant social—and perhaps also political—force over the next decades."

While demand shrinks for some specialties and immediate crises create unemployment (as happened after 9-11), job creation goes on, and wealth is generated. This continues in times of peace and war, overcoming interruptions. The overall process of renewal and innovation forces the work force to adjust, to renew its skills, and to move out of unproductive industries and into more productive ones. As the steel industry lost market share to more technologically advanced nations, it was forced to shed hundreds of thousands of jobs in the second half of the twentieth century. At the same time, millions of Americans found jobs in various computer-related functions, from building and maintaining computers to using them at work.

Whole new industries emerged where they did not exist before. Software development is a recent example; it did not exist as a profit-making industry before the mid-1960s. Companies that make DNA-based products are up-to-date examples of wealth and job creation. History's lesson is that there will be more as technology leads to new goods and services which lead to new enterprises and new jobs. In the process, individual Americans, companies, and the country as a whole benefit in a win-win scenario. What it takes is deeply ingrained in the American experience of seeking economic opportunities as summed up by a leading figure in creative thinking, Edward de Bono: "Everyone is surrounded by opportunities. But they only exist once they have been seen. And they will only be seen if they are looked for."

CHAPTER 7

FROM OUR LEADERS

The secret of a leader lies in the tests he has faced over the whole course of his life and the habit of action he develops in meeting those tests.

GAIL SHEEHY

S hortly before 10 A.M. on September 11, aboard United Flight 93, a cell phone relayed the final words of a 32-year-old account manager for the Oracle Corporation. What had started out as his routine trip to a San Francisco meeting had become a confrontation with hijackers aiming the Boeing 757 at Washington, D.C., with the White House or the Capitol as likely targets. Several passengers banded together "to do something about it [the hijacking]" as one of them told his wife over a cell phone. In the final minutes, the account manager, Todd Beamer, recited the 23rd Psalm with a GTE operator—"Yea, though I walk through the Valley of the Shadow of Death, I shall fear no evil; for Thou art with me...."

A call to action by Beamer against enemies of America were his last words and the last heard from the plane: "Are you guys ready? Let's roll."

The statement deserves to stand with others in the American tradition of devotion to God and country, along-side "I only regret that I have but one life to lose for my country" (Nathan Hale's last words in 1776, before the British hanged him as a spy). Beamer's words are contemporary, but the underlying significance the same. The episode affirms a tradition of leadership and heroism—linked in our national experience as a source of strength in tough times. It is part of realistic optimism to acknowledge the linkage and to count on it in moving the nation forward.

The qualities of leadership and heroism embedded in the national experience are all-inclusive, ranging from the so-called average American to the men and women in positions of power. We look to heroes and leaders, and respond best to a combination of both. It is part of a deep-seated sense of equality and expectation for all Americans. We are all equal and equally responsible when a call to action is sounded. In the perceptive 1831 verdict of Alexis de Tocqueville: "The government of democracy brings the notion of political rights to the level of the humblest citizens, just as the dissemination of wealth brings the notion of property within the reach of all the members of the community."

Particularly in times of crisis, the nation counts on both leadership and heroism to emerge from all levels of the citizenry—from individuals who rise to the occasion to business and political leaders who show us the way ahead. That is a lasting significance of the 9-11 catastrophe: the harvest of leadership and heroism from all directions. Heroism and leadership merged when men and women who had reported for a usual day's work suddenly found themselves risking their lives to lead others to safety, responding alongside firefighters and police officers. Heroism became everyone's challenge. Leadership became anyone's role.

This potential response from all Americans is a formidable resource, given the nature of the war on terrorism which knows no boundaries, leaves no one a bystander, and makes everyone potentially a participant, a combatant, a victim, a leader. Each time terrorists attack, the dimensions of their all-inclusive warfare confront everyone on the receiving end, in or out of uniform, in positions of authority or as an "accidental" leader. Everyone is involved because terrorists can attack:

ANYONE

We are all potential victims as terrorists strike to create terror, as well as to wreak havoc and destruction. Accidents of time and place can put any of us in the line of fire as circumstances call for action on our part. We can be sipping takeout coffee at our desks, riding the elevator, sitting in the window seat of a hijacked plane. Or we can respond in our line of duty as a firefighter, police officer, or ambulance driver. By its very nature, the terrorism we face is indiscriminate in waging war and indifferent to the casualty count.

ANYTIME

Given the nature of terrorism, terrorists have complete freedom of choice in deciding when they act. In fact, as they demonstrate, the element of surprise is a powerful weapon, with as many variations as terrorists can devise and take advantage of. The uncertainty bred by terrorism magnifies the impact of individual actions by a What next? factor.

ANYWHERE

Terrorists have demonstrated that there are no limits to what their ingenuity and imagination will think up in a world without insurmountable boundaries, geographical, technical, or logistical. There are no completely safe areas. No place is out of bounds, off limits. What terrorists target—no matter where—they can conceivably hit, national leaders included.

Anyone-anytime-anywhere terrorism honors no limits and brings its war to everyone. On 9-11, the heroes who risked and lost their lives helping others and those who survived faced the unexpected and the life-threatening without advance notice. Suddenly, they were in the middle of a war, without any separation between combatants and noncombatants. When the mayor of New York, Rudy Giuliani, rushed to the scene, he was in the heat of battle, as much as the Earl of Cardigan directing the legendary charge of the Light Brigade in the Crimean War. So were the individual men and women working in the Twin Towers who came to work and found themselves in the middle of a terrorist attack.

LEADING THE WAY

In the heat of battle, leaders emerge when they fill a gap, meet a need, aim at results. They take the initiative. They literally take the lead and have done so in the current stage of terrorism, where any and all Americans can face a life-and-death situation. Todd Beamer, for one. The mayor of New York City, for another. Both of them demonstrated leadership when face to face with terrorism and reminded us of the human resources available in America as part of our response to terror. But to take into account what we need and want from leadership, we also must include ongoing leadership that does not involve life-and-death heroism. It is the leadership of Americans in all levels of government and Americans who run or help to run enterprises of all kinds. They face crises of a different kind in the competitive world of business, where the stakes nonetheless carry weight: economic survival for individual men and women and their families. To tap this source of insight into leadership, we include highlights of a conversation with the remarkable, down-to-earth president and CEO of SRC Holdings Corporation based in Springfield, Missouri—Jack Stack. After leading a floundering enterprise back from the brink of disaster, he heads a successful organization with 16 holdings and subsidiaries and is the mastermind behind a highly regarded approach called *open-book management*. Close-ups of Beamer, Giuliani, and Stack as leaders lay the groundwork for an inventory of what we want and need from leadership to emerge stronger as a people and as a nation.

To start with Beamer, he embodied grass-roots American verities and strengths, bonded as he was to church and family, committed to his job, enthusiastic about sports as both player and fan. Todd and his wife, Lisa, taught the senior high school Sunday school class at Princeton Alliance Church, and for good measure, he played on the church softball team. An avid and indiscriminate Chicago fan, he turned the family game room into a temple devoted to the Cubs, Bulls, and Bears, including a Cubs pinball machine.

At Christian High School in Wheaton, Illinois, he played baseball, basketball, and soccer, and when his family moved West, he continued playing in school sports in his senior year at a California high school, while also making the honor society. He went on to attend Fresno State University with a dream of playing professional baseball but changed schools when he realized that the dream was beyond reach. He returned home to Illinois and attended Wheaton College, a coed Christian College northeast of Chicago. There, in a senior seminar, he met his wife, Lisa. They were married in 1994 after he earned an MBA from DePaul University in Chicago and settled in Princeton, New Jersey.

From all accounts, Todd was a star performer for Oracle, a go-getter who was on his cell phone constantly. Earlier in the year, as a top salesman, he earned a five-day trip to Italy with his wife. Even though he had to travel as many as four times a month, sometimes for a week, he made every effort to be at home with his family. In fact, instead of leaving for a business trip to California on Monday, September 10, he left early on September 11 so he could spend the previous evening with his expectant wife and two young sons (four and two years old).

The details of what happened on Flight 93 after Todd called other passengers to action will never be known, but they undoubtedly made a major difference. The hijackers never reached their target. In calling the Flight 93 resisters heroes, FBI Special Agent Andy Black added, that "From what we know, this plane was headed for another strategic target." Vice President Dick Cheney credited the action with foiling an attack on Washington: "Without question, the attack would've been much worse if it hadn't been for the courageous actions of those individuals on United 93."

The most compelling depiction was delivered by Todd's widow in affirming that heroes live on and in showing how to find meaning in tragedy. "Some people live their whole lives, long lives, without having left anything behind. My sons will be told their whole lives that their father was a hero, that he saved lives. It's a great legacy for a father to leave his children." Her defiance of terrorism and determination to carry on went further. In the days after 9-11, Lisa Beamer took the same Newark-to-San Francisco Flight 93 and met with the associates Todd had been on his way to see. They discussed fund-raising for the Todd M. Beamer Foundation, dedicated to helping the 22 children who lost parents on the flight. Her hope: that those children will grow into the kind of people who "can make courageous and moral decisions."

The Beamers are part of a continuum of heroism and leadership whose foundation is the lives and moral posture of millions of Americans who, unnoticed, go about lives of commitment, on call to become heroes and leaders. At the other end of the continuum, as a designated office holder who captured worldwide attention, Rudy Giuliani transcended his position as Mayor of New York City. He spoke for all Americans in capturing the spirit of resistance, as when he told an anxious populace, "The thing we have to do is demonstrate that the spirit of New York City is not its buildings. Buildings are important, but the spirit of New York is its people, free people dedicated to democracy."

At funeral service after funeral service that he attended, Giuliani looked to the future, to the same legacy that Lisa Beamer described, to the strength that the next generation will provide. In naming Giuliani "Person of the Year," *Time* magazine recorded the message he repeated to the children of 9-11 heroes as they buried their fathers. Congregations wept as he honored the fallen and comforted their families, finding strength in their sorrow. "Nobody can take your father from you. He is part of you. He helped make you— He's with you—nobody can take him away from you. You have something lots of children don't have. You have the absolute, certain knowledge that your dad was a great man."

From the time he rushed from midtown Manhattan to the World Trade Center, Giuliani was in the middle of what was happening. He emerged as the leader who directed the response to the 9-11 attack in tactical terms and inspired New Yorkers (as well as the entire country) as a hero who risked his own life when buildings collapsed all around him. In that one dreaded morning, he became, as *Time* rightly pointed out, homeland security boss, decision maker, crisis manager, consoler in chief, "global symbol of healing and defiance." He defined the situation and identified the challenge. And millions listened. "Tomorrow, New York is going to be here. And we're going to rebuild, and we're going to be stronger than we were before.... I want the people of New York to be an example to the rest of the country, and the rest of the world, that terrorism can't stop us." Polls confirmed that his rallying cry was heard. Gallup reported that 90 percent of Americans agreed that the way New Yorkers "responded to the attacks on September 11 helped rally the rest of the country;" 94 percent felt Giuliani had done a very good/good job responding to the 9-11 attacks.

New York's police commissioner, Bernard Kerik, who was at the mayor's side, described what Giuliani's leadership meant to New Yorkers. It was very personal. "He is almost like God. People are coming up to him crying, thanking him for being there. All they want to do is make him say it's gonna be okay. And that's exactly what he does."

Giuliani had a role model of leadership fixed in his mind—Winston Churchill and the people of London during the Blitz in 1940. It enabled him to focus on the resource that terrorism attacks and that leadership taps, the spirit of the people. By his words, his presence, his visibility, he exhibited what *Time* magazine rightly identified as "eloquence under fire" that made him "a global symbol of healing and defiance."

Churchill biographer Roy Jenkins, whose chapters on World War II inspired Giuliani in his response to 9-11, summed up the mayor's leadership. "What Giuliani succeeded in doing is what Churchill succeeded in doing in the dreadful summer of 1940: He managed to create an illusion that we were bound to win."

In leading the city, Giuliani demonstrated know-how, skill in delegation, and sound decision making. He stands out as a leader to be studied and analyzed in his own right. He knows New York as a quintessential product of the city, a tough prosecutor, and a no-nonsense commander of its various departments. As Mayor, his daily 8 A.M. staff meetings became the basis for 9-11 problem-solving sessions. He demonstrated the ability to cut through protocol and to single out strong choices for important, high-ranking positions. He demonstrated leadership in making the streets safer and cleaner, a dramatic turnaround that made all the difference in the world to New Yorkers, from subway straphangers to limousine liberals. After 9-11, it became clear that the city whose residents proudly call the greatest in the world was led not only by a mayor who got things done, but one who has "a tremendously huge heart" (in the words of his police commissioner).

He also blends optimism with an unerring sense of realism. When hearing someone say that Americans began living in a different world after 9-11, he made a significant correction. He sees the same world as before, but now, as he points out, we recognize the threats and the dangers. "So," Giuliani says, "it's probably a safer world now."

A BUSINESS CASE

In addition to personal heroism in an emergency and political leadership under fire, America has an ongoing resource in day-in, day-out leadership in the world of business. Like the proverbial iceberg where only the tip is visible, every business enterprise is filled with decision makers who make the difference between competing successfully and being left behind, between profit and loss. In countless everyday activities—from sales and service personnel and first-line managers to CEOs—leadership-based decisions accumulate, making an enterprise healthy or unhealthy. In major decision making at upper levels of organizations, those in positions of authority can make or break an enterprise.   Like generals on the battlefield, their choices and decisions win or lose battles and, ultimately, wars. In the battlefield of competition, their lieutenants make specific decisions that carry the enterprise forward. At the end of the day, the inexorable scorecard of profit and loss separates winners and losers.

What makes Jack Stack a prototype of leadership is his success in turning around a seemingly doomed enterprise into what *Inc* magazine has called "one of America's most competitive small companies" (in a country where 99 percent of all businesses are small businesses). What he does is quintessentially American in the way he mobilizes the know-how and commitment of more than 1,000 employees, then spreads his gospel of "open-book management." His success story represents and typifies American leadership in all its manifestations. It happens all the time in America, though the crisis and the uncertainty that confronted Stack and his employees warranted little attention outside a failing operation in Missouri. But to the employees involved it was world-shaking—in their very real world of having a job, paying the bills, raising a family.

A LEADERSHIP INVENTORY

Leaving aside a debate on whether leaders are made or born, creatures of circumstance or makers of their own destiny, we know them when we experience them, and we do not forget what they are like and their impact on us. Whether "accidental" or officially designated, leaders are immediately recognizable. We know what we expect from them, never more so than in times of crisis. As is clear by now, we are confident that America has an ample reservoir of leadership to draw upon, from the "average" American to those men and women who are "in charge" at various levels of organizations, enterprises, and governmental units.

In discussing leadership, an advance disclaimer is called for. Leadership has an "X factor," making it more than a simple summary of its parts. As Warren Bennis has stated after extensive and authoritative research on the subject,

"Like everyone else, [leaders] are the sum of all their experiences. Unlike most people, however, each of them amounts to more than the sum, because they have made more of their experiences. These are originals, not copies." Bennis adds a comment worth heeding in citing a statement by the French cubist painter, Georges Braque: "The only thing that matters in art can't be explained." Bennis adds that "the same might be said of leadership."

Nonetheless, we know that leaders are expected to deliver tangible results. If we expect and need leadership—and all of American history demonstrates that we do and that it works—it is important to understand what we want from leaders, what we can expect, no more, no less. Looking ahead, with leadership needed at all levels of society, we as individuals owe leaders our support, but not uncritical support. All the while, let's beware of opportunists disguising themselves as leaders, particularly purveyors of quick fixes, sellers of simplicity, deniers of real problems, peddlers of scapegoating. Such a warning is called for, though in our view, reality and the facts catch up with and expose charlatans if they do not give themselves away by going too far in what they say and/or do.

OPTIMISM

We have already stressed optimism as a key element of leadership. It stands to reason that only fanatics follow pessimists and that positive leadership improves the odds and optimizes the possibilities. People would rather be led by someone who appeals to the brighter side of things than to the negative. This is not to suggest that good leaders avoid negative realities. When Churchill led the British during World War II, he had plenty of negatives to deal with, not the least of which was the almost daily bombardment of London by the Germans. He did not ignore the horror of the bombing, while appealing to the strengths of his fellow Londoners, as he did on Britain's darkest day in the last half-millennium, when British soldiers were driven into the sea at Dunkirk in June 1940, the same month that France came under Nazi control. His talent for recognizing the negative while betting on the positive is epitomized by what he said to his fellow Britons.

> We shall not flag or fail. We shall go on to the end. We shall fight in France, we shall fight on the seas and oceans, we shall fight with growing confidence and growing strength in the air, we shall defend our island, whatever the cost may be, we shall fight on the beaches, we shall fight on the landing grounds, we shall fight in the fields and in the streets, we shall fight in the hills; we shall never surrender.

In Britain's darkest day, Churchill essentially said, "We will prevail, though it's far from over and it requires an all-out effort."

If optimism is essential in any leader, we should look for that characteristic and demand it of our political leaders.

Out with naysayers, complainers, and those who obsess over problems instead of pursuing and proposing solutions. New York's mayor did not complain when the Trade Towers were destroyed; he told the world that the city and the nation would overcome the problems created by the disaster. America would recover, and the city and country would be better for it. As individuals, we have an obligation to look for the positive side of things, for opportunities to support improvements, to volunteer and take part. We know how corrosive negative attitudes can be in our lives and at work. If ever there was a time to put them aside, this is it.

REALISM

Particularly in tough times, we need leaders who face facts in what they do and what they say. Double-talk and false promises create doubt, which only compounds the uncertainty that everyone already feels in times of crisis. Stack makes a point of identifying himself as a realist—someone who "looks for the upside and manages for the downside." In the 9-11 crisis, Secretary of Defense Donald Rumsfeld overcame misgivings about his leadership by not exaggerating successes or minimizing setbacks. As *The Economist* said of him approvingly: "He either speaks straightforwardly, or not at all." The *Wall Street Journal* cited Churchill in reporting on the role of realism in times of turmoil:

During tough times, it takes leaders who are frank and compassionate, as well as decisive, to inspire others. When Winston Churchill during the dark days of World War II told his countrymen that "the news from France is bad," he won their trust with his bluntness and sustained their determination to keep fighting. In a similar vein, corporate executives who are honest about their companies' performance and who acknowledge the sacrifices they are asking employees to make are more likely to muster loyalty than those who withhold information and praise.

ACTION

To make a difference, leadership requires a commitment to action. Churchill's Dunkirk speech is full of resolution about what his nation had to do and would do. His eloquent statement left no doubt about his call to action—an all-out effort, his way of saying, "Let's roll." Good leaders constantly emphasize their commitment to action. In a radio broadcast a month after commenting on Dunkirk, he said it again: "We shall defend every village, every town, and every city."

"Doing something" is a formula for success in both war and peace, in any situation defined as competitive, in any confrontation where there are winners and losers. It is as American as the Washington Monument, and the examples are endless, like footnotes that overwhelm the main text of the American story. As a prototype illustration of what we mean, there is the Jack Stack story. In the early 1980s, he was about to become a leader without followers, faced with closing down the plant he managed for International Harvester and, thus, laying off 250 people. Stack takes such stakes personally, and his feelings emerge when he talks as the man in charge and responsible. The prospect of layoffs kept him up at night; he was "all tensed up," he lay in bed, staring at the ceiling. Then he made his decision. He recalls what he said to himself, "Hell, leaders at least try to do something." He proceeded to talk to all the plant employees—on factory floors, in the lunchroom, in bars— meeting the problem head-on: "Should we try to save the plant and not just sit there like a bunch of wimps?" The answer was a resounding yes to saving the plant by buying it.

Stack put together $100,000 and leveraged it to get an $8.9 million bank loan: "We were one of the worst-leveraged buyouts of the eighties. Our debt-to-equity ratio was 89 to one." Starting February 1, 1983, the newly independent Springfield ReManufacturing Company (SRC) had a $90,000 interest payment to meet on the first day of every month. Not surprisingly, its stock was priced at 10 cents in a field crowded with competitors remanufacturing engines and their components and manufacturing power units, generators, starters, alternators, and electrical components. In 10 years, the $100,000 purchase was worth $25 million; by the early 1990s, the initial 10-cent stock soared by 20,000 percent to $20, with 80 percent of it owned by employees. They became more than stockholders and employees.

They became fully informed participants, educated in what business is all about. They were taught how to read income statements and balance sheets, and they learned how their work and their on-the-job decisions contributed to the bottom line. The SRC approach became a heralded system for employee involvement, open-book management, that has been picked up by companies of all sizes.

Stack as SRC's president and CEO embodies leadership with his quintessential American approach of full employee participation and proactive leadership. His view of leadership in uncertain times gets down to basics:

> A leader has to worry about what could go wrong, always worrying about where the other shoe is going to fall, always asking, What if? Leaders need to consider contingencies in their thinking all the time. They need to think like strategists. In uncertain times, leaders must have courage and confidence, and they must have a long-term view. People want to go somewhere, and they'll follow you if you can paint a picture, present a process for getting through uncertainty. Forecasting is absolutely critical. You want to make the right decisions on a day-to-day, month-to-month, year-to-year basis and communicate that to everybody. That's vital.

DELEGATION

In analyses of successful leaders, the skill of delegation comes to the fore, particularly in the memoirs of the people close to them. By sharing responsibility and distributing assignments, leaders extend their reach and multiply their effectiveness. In the process, they capitalize on the knowledge and know-how of others and rely on surrogate eyes and ears to stay on top of what is going on. Effective leaders set an example, show people what to do, inspire courage, and make sure the necessary wherewithal is provided. In Churchill's case, he translated the call to "fight them on the beaches" into a full-scale effort to raise, train, and equip a large British military force of naval, army, and air units to defend the country. He let his cabinet members figure out the details and deliver results. "It's amazing," President Truman said, "what you can accomplish if you do not care who gets the credit."

Delegation is a hallmark of American presidents in wartime (except for James Madison in the War of 1812). Lincoln, Wilson, Roosevelt, Truman, Johnson, and both Bush presidents delegated responsibility and considerable authority to their generals to lead the fighting. Anyone who has worked in an organization will identify the best managers as the ones who give everyone the space to do their work and get their jobs done. Micromanagers are the bane of men and women trying to do the best possible job in any organization, whereas managers who lead by trusting people and leaving them free to succeed get the best results. What America needs (and produces) is leadership that leverages the skill and initiative of individuals and organizations to do the work of the nation.

The entire process of delegation revolves around trust, initiative, and commitment. We must trust each other to do what's expected by drawing on our training, experience, and know-how to do what's needed. The heroism and individual leadership that emerged from 9-11 became a cumulative demonstration of initiative, a distinctive American trait that showed up on 9-11 in countless individual acts directed at the overriding goal of saving lives. In times of crisis, commitment is second nature when the cause is believed in, thereby producing the 9-11 effect. New Yorkers, then people from all over the country and even the world rushed to help, becoming followers or leaders, as circumstances required.

Jack Stack describes what he would do if suddenly made leader of another organization:

> I'd be delegating leadership so fast it'd make your head spin.... I would immediately try to delegate everything there was about leadership and to show people what it is all about. I would tell them what my job is and what the responsibilities are. I would try to get across to them the belief that if I could do this, then they could, too. I think you've got to get people involved in the decision-making process. They must be able to establish standards, benchmarks, roles and accountability, knowing full well what the risks are. A leader is a teacher and ignites followers, gets people to participate.

COMMUNICATION

A positive attitude, coupled with a bias for action, is not enough. Leaders must articulate what is to be done in ways that build confidence and stir people to action. We demand of our leaders that they "speak" to us, and we have the responsibility to answer—by speaking up in our communities, attending city council hearings, writing letters to the editor, participating in community organizations. The more feedback and the more dialogue, the more effective the leadership.

Some of the greatest moments in the history of leadership center on effective communications. Kennedy's "Ask not what your country can do for you—ask what you can do for your country" is classic. President Ronald Reagan is cherished as a leader because of his outstanding ability to get his message across on television and in person. There were many things he did not do well, but his limitations were set aside because he was "The Great Communicator."

Churchill, one of the greatest communicators in European history, was a man in deep trouble politically for many years. He made many military mistakes in World War I that essentially kept him out of politics in the 1920s and 1930s. When he became prime minister in the early days of World War II, Germany was winning big, conquering all of Western Europe and driving the British off the continent at Dunkirk. London was being bombed and battered; the British Isles faced invasion. By all accounts, Churchill could be put down at that time as a loser leading a losing cause. Today, we honor him as a history-making leader. Why? He was determined, he was lucky, and the U.S. entered the war, but all along he was also a compelling communicator whose rhetoric became a powerful weapon.

Cold quotes do not do justice to the sound of Churchill's voice, to his cadence, to his rhetorical command. It was not only the words, but the way he delivered them. To the British public he said, "Let us...brace ourselves to our duties, and so bear ourselves that if the British Empire and its Commonwealth last for a thousand years, men will still say, 'This was their finest hour.'" To Americans he said, "Give us the tools, and we will finish the job." After the war, to a world grappling with the rise of Communism, he labeled and influenced four tense decades of history with his statement, "From Stettin in the Baltic to Trieste in the Adriatic, an iron curtain has descended across the continent."

What better advisor on communication than Churchill: "If you have an important point to make, don't try to be subtle or clever. Use a pile driver. Hit the point once. Then come back and hit it again. Then hit it again with a tremendous whack."

RISK TAKING

There is a very human reason why it is easier to follow than to lead. There is much less risk. Leaders are out in front, targets for everything from negative criticism to emotion-charged opposition, from vilification to physical attacks. So what should we do? When leaders take a risk on our behalf, in politics or business, we can get behind them or at least give them the benefit of the doubt. When we disagree, we can make a point of offering constructive criticism and search out alternative lines of action. If we agree, we can support the effort and find ways to help out. We can also take the initiative by standing up and speaking out, at the risk of facing criticism by taking an unpopular stand. All in all, the fewer the people on the sidelines, the greater the chance of sound decision making behind any risk.

In a time of uncertainty, our leaders must make decisions fraught with risk. If solutions were obvious and decisions incontrovertible, little or no risk is involved. But that seldom is the case in the real world. Between risks that are lottery long shots and those with high probabilities, there is a risk/return barometer. The higher the risk, the greater the return, also the greater the price of failing. So we all need to be realistic about risk taking. We cannot expect that our leaders will never make a mistake. But we can expect that they avoid repeating them and that we all learn—bystanders, participants, and leaders—by examining past mistakes to avoid future ones.

In a celebrated example of risk taking by a national leader, President Kennedy told the nation he wanted to put a man on the moon in 10 years, though many of his advisors urged him not to go out on a limb. However, he also had many in the scientific community inside and outside of government assuring him it was not beyond America's capability, though a great deal needed to be invented. So he took the risk. Earlier in his administration, he took another risk in which he had not done his homework. He approved the invasion of Cuba by exiles, which became the humiliating Bay of Pigs fiasco. In Kennedy's case, the Bay of Pigs happened first—and failed—while the commitment to the moon landing succeeded. After the Bay of Pigs, he might have decided not to stick his neck out again, but that would not have been the Kennedy that the nation admired and celebrated as a leader.

In response to 9-11, President George W. Bush faced up to the risks that suddenly confronted him. He risked a challenge to civil liberties to clamp down on America's enemies with his Homeland Defense initiative and risked that he could build and maintain a worldwide coalition long enough to win the war on terrorism. It would have been easier to bomb terrorist camps, inflict casualties, and declare victory—and he might have gotten away with it. Instead, he opted for the high road: reconstructing a nation devastated by two decades of war (an echo of the Marshall Plan to promote European recovery after World War II).

EMPATHY

Optimism, a determination to take action, effective communications, ability to delegate, and a willingness to take risks are not enough. We need to add a characteristic that has enriched the quality of life in America: empathy for others. This nation's religious beliefs are grounded in concepts of charity, its identity shaped by a tradition of helping each other and of neighborliness. In clinical terms, it is called *empathy*. It means understanding how someone else feels and registering the pain and suffering of others, both near and far. It also means understanding someone else's motives and point of view. Americans at their best tolerate differences and respond to those in need, traits that are tested and challenged in times of uncertainty.

Despite all the criticism and second-guessing of U.S. foreign policy, no other country surpasses America's capacity to respond to suffering and disaster anywhere in the world. Whenever there is a natural disaster, America can be counted on to fly in medicine, blankets, tents, and food. What nation in modern times declared war on poverty in launching Great Society programs? What country fights its enemy, then "bombs" the countryside with food? We would argue that empathy deserves attention as a major source of strength for the United States. It is a national asset, both internally and externally, that grows in value during times of crisis.

In the wake of 9-11, Americans all over the country felt empathy for 9-11 victims and their families, and sought ways to help in whatever way possible. Empathy unites the nation as much as the determination to crush its enemies.

Empathy mobilizes our desire to take action and prompts us to respond to leadership. In turn, we expect our leaders to demonstrate empathy, to sympathize with those in need, and to show that they "have heart." That quality in Giuliani won over the nation and struck a worldwide chord. He was "strong enough to let his voice brim with pain, compassion and love," *Time* magazine reported. "When he said, 'the number of casualties will be more than any of us can bear,' he showed a side of himself most people had never seen." As New York's police commissioner, Kerik, noted, Giuliani showed his "tremendously huge heart."

STRAIGHT TALK

Finally, we have the *modus operandi* that is special for Americans: straight talk. Nothing goes more against the national grain than obvious double-talk. It is un-American. Leaders who cannot be believed lose their following, especially when they demand sacrifices, no matter how gifted they are or how righteous their cause. Double-talk's bedfellow, hypocrisy, compromises credibility and undermines trust. One way to eliminate the risk of hypocrisy and thereby minimize the risk of losing credibility is to "tell it like it is." When leaders believe what they say and say what they believe, people don't just listen. They follow.

President Roosevelt's singular impact was personified by his "fireside" chats on the radio during the Depression and World War II. Each American felt as though he was speaking to him or her personally and telling it like it is. He acknowledged the difficulty of eliminating the Depression and creating more jobs, and told Americans what he was doing to confront the nation's problems. During World War II, he spelled out what Americans faced and what was being done. He did not hesitate to talk about the sacrifices needed and the effort demanded.

Clearly, what we need and, based on America's history, what we can expect from our leaders is straight talk. We should, in turn, take our own medicine when we dialogue, whether we agree or disagree, all the time remembering that straight talk alone is an orphan. Separated from commitment and action, it is only talk. It proves itself in action, whether we lead or follow. There is a time for debate, and there are times when we must get behind our leaders. It is a delicately balanced tension in America because of our commitment to civil liberties and individualism and the high value we place on cooperation. The challenge for all Americans is to demonstrate the capacity to follow and to lead, knowing when to choose one or the other. Together, leading and following point to a body of practices and attitudes that back up a winning bet on America's future after 9-11. How to place that bet is the theme of the final chapter.

A NATIONAL AND PERSONAL AGENDA

*Let every nation know, whether it wishes us
well or ill, that we shall pay any price, bear
any burden, meet any hardship, support any
friend, oppose any foe to assure the survival
and the success of liberty.*

PRESIDENT JOHN F. KENNEDY, 1961

When President Kennedy said those words at his
inauguration on January 20, 1961, the United States was in
the midst of the Cold War. Fidel Castro and Cuba, just 90
miles off the shores of America, was a hotbed of Communism; China seemed destined to dominate Asia; the Soviet
Union and the U.S. hovered on the brink of nuclear disaster.
In his thousand days in office, Kennedy approved an invasion of Cuba, nearly experienced World War III during the
Cuban Missile Crisis, and made fateful decisions that committed his nation to a decade of warfare in a little-known
area of the world called Vietnam.

His was also a time when the nation committed itself to putting a man on the moon and to the largest expansion of education, from kindergarten through university, in the history of the nation. Kennedy's successor, Lyndon B. Johnson, built on this momentum by progressing with his Great Society programs. As individuals, Americans served in the Peace Corps, went to college in record numbers, joined the military, participated in an expanding economy, and helped give birth to the Information Age.

The story of America, as embedded in the inaugural words, revolves around a body of practices that emphasizes freedom for the individual and liberty as a national commitment. On the one hand, there has always been the special role of government in fostering liberty and national welfare, while on the other hand, Americans have taken personal responsibility for their individual success. So it was in 1961 and so is it in the new normalcy. The frame of mind is thoroughly American. We think the great French commentator on the American scene, Alexis de Tocqueville (1805–1859), hit the right note when he wrote in 1835 that Americans "have all a lively faith in the perfectibility of man, they judge that the diffusion of knowledge must necessarily be advantageous, and the consequences of ignorance fatal; they all consider society as a changing scene, in which nothing is, or ought to be, permanent; and they admit that what appears to them today to be good, may be superseded by something better tomorrow."

Combine that optimism with determination, and we have the makings of a commitment to a way of life and a set of values that can stand strong against terrorists. America's history is on its side. From its beginnings, the nation has applied effectively its values and practices, accumulating the wherewithal to make it the most powerful nation on earth. Forty years later, it is easier today to display and act on Kennedy's resolve than it was in 1961. The link between the determination and resources to grow, to protect, and to impose is greater today than in any other time in American history.

The current response to our Black Tuesday in September hearkens back to the tense time prior to the start of the Civil War, when Americans all over the country sensed a national crisis. A new president had just barely been elected by a sharply divided electorate without any mandate from the American public to implement a specific agenda. When he left his home town of Springfield, Illinois on February 11, 1861 to assume his duties as president— just two months before the start of the American Civil War—Abraham Lincoln sensed what lay ahead and shared his thoughts with neighbors and well-wishers as he boarded his train. He could just as easily have been speaking to Americans after 9-11: "Let us have faith that right makes might, and in that faith let us to the end dare to do our duty as we understand it."

The advice holds up today. While headlines and news bulletins can distract us from the way we go about our daily lives, the basics endure, along with Lincoln's advice in the face of news on the negative side. Admittedly, the press had no choice in reporting the economic consequences of 9-11, when over 600,000 people lost their jobs and when, in the week following 9-11, the stock market dropped faster than it had since the Great Depression. At the end of 2001, the journalistic ritual of making lists accented the negative. One example among many was the CNN/Money list of the year's top 10 business stories.   Only one—number 10—was a positive one, dealing with the increased sales of houses.

Yet in the end, that may have been the most revealing story of all, because people do not buy houses if they do not want homes, if they do not believe in the brightness of their personal economic future, if they do not want a way of life that includes family, personal comfort, and physical security. The jobs lost because of 9-11 and the recession of 2001 will be replaced, as they have in the past. The stock market bounced back from 9-11 and will respond to the overall economic health of the nation.

Meanwhile, Americans go about the serious business of finding jobs, having babies, getting an education, buying houses, and rallying to the national determination to eradicate terrorism. The mundane tasks of daily life are seen for their importance to our lives as Americans and for their role in national recovery and renewal. Amidst a surge of patriotism, the real story of the new normalcy is the combination of public and private initiatives, rooted in basic national values and laced with a solid dose of optimism. If one wanted a single, specific "to do" from this book, it is simply to embrace what has always served the nation well, to do as New York Mayor Rudy Giuliani advocates, "Go about your lives," "Be normal."

In this book, we have explored the implications of personal responsibility and actions, and their effects on how Americans think and feel. We have done the same with regard to government's role. In the end, America's historical experience suggests that what individuals do collectively has a greater effect on the welfare of this nation than do government programs. What we do as individuals is important. We have argued that what is now essential is a renewed acceptance of personal initiative to ensure our own security and that of our communities, a security not made of more guns but of more tolerance of each other, more jobs, a better economy, and more commitment to national ideals, tempered with pragmatism. Ours is not a call to run out and buy M-16 rifles. It is a call to be prudent and observant, to demonstrate commitment and a sense of responsibility, to call upon public officials and community organizations to be responsive to the needs of the nation. Ours is not a call just for national economic recovery programs—Washington will do that, anyway—but for individuals to rise to the occasion through personal initiatives, a heightened sense of commitment, and an unremitting demand that our leaders respond to the needs of the country and its people.

FEAR CONQUERED AND THINGS TO DO

There is no question but that Americans felt exposed, vulnerable to danger, and personally at risk as a result of 9-11. This showed up in national polls, the many calls to local officials about mail suspected of anthrax contamination, and the suspicion directed at young Arab Americans. A wartime atmosphere prevailed. After all, thousands of civilians had died as a result of one day's terrorism and tens of thousands in the armed services went off to war. All initiatives and responses to the new normalcy were held hostage by the threat of terrorism and the demands of security.

Two fundamental sets of issues are at stake regarding security: getting back into operation after the attacks and protecting people and property, assets and information. While for years major corporations and government agencies had a range of physical security and backup programs in place, most smaller organizations did not. Cost considerations and lack of focus usually accounted for failures to provide security and backups. All that changed after 9-11, as organizations reviewed their security arrangements or set them up when and where they were lacking. The lessons that stand out are:

1. Concentrating employees in a single facility (as happened in New York) or a whole department in one wing (as at the Pentagon) proved to be a serious mistake when disaster struck. A "headquarters mentality" of centralizing company operations shifted even further toward telecommuting and working at home or in satellite locations

2. The Internet did not go down, although many internal networks and phone systems did. Therefore, organizations will probably rely more on the Internet in the years to come. Decentralization of assets and work is emerging as a strategy to improve security.

3. Not enough backup arrangements for data and computing had been made by affected businesses. Those who can will remedy this situation.

4. A bigger problem was that too few firms had made backup arrangements for new offices and terminals to use in the days immediately following 9-11. One would think this problem could be easily fixed, but it is actually complex and expensive.

5. There are limits to physical security. Guards at entrances to buildings and ID badges are no match for anthrax, airplanes crashing into buildings, or nuclear waste detonated on a city street. Nonethe-

less, a great deal is already being done to beef up low- and high-tech security systems.

Given these five lessons, what can be done? Implicit in these lessons is a sixth, that organizations, not individuals, can have a greater positive impact on security than can individuals acting alone. At the public level, local, state, and federal government can do much more than organizations responding on a solo basis, as significant as that can be. Three responses come to the fore. First, organizations are focusing on backup and contingency plans that ensure that their work continues after a terrorist attack. Second, they are implementing time-honored practices in information backup. Third, they are enhancing the physical security of buildings, vehicles, and employees.

If you accept the notion that security is more than protecting Americans from injury, the focus on organized and coordinated efforts makes considerable sense. For one thing, as a matter of national policy, we need to take into account the impact of job loss, not only on a breadwinner but also on his or her family. The impact is economic, psychological, and social, a trying experience only fully grasped with first-hand experience. From a national viewpoint, unemployment threatens the well-being of the country and its ability to function. Widespread economic trouble for individual Americans saps the country's strengths and its ability to recover from disasters and terrorist attacks.

To ensure the continuance of business as close as possible to "usual," company managements must develop answers to the operational question, If my building is blown up, where do my surviving employees go to work the next day? Facilities can be acquired or rented as a contingency, or other company office sites can be prepared to accept an influx of employees. Firms are also spreading their employees out across a city, the nation, or multiple buildings, so that if one part goes down, employees elsewhere in the company know how to carry on. Long before a crisis, responses can be ready, in place, fully rehearsed.

Setting up physical backup sites for employees with the proper equipment raises the question, Where do we do this and how? It was a staggering problem after 9-11. IBM employees working with customers in setting up new data centers found that the problem was not technology but locating space all over New York and New Jersey. One IBM executive involved in that process, Todd Gordon, summed up the challenge: "It's been a physical problem, not a technological one."

THE ROLE OF INFORMATION AND PHYSICAL SECURITY

After 40 years of preaching backup to companies, many in the information technology (IT) industry are seeing a surge of interest in the subject. The key steps are fairly straightforward. Make sure that whatever backup information a company needs is set up elsewhere, ready to use, and that the appropriate people are aware of such information and have access to it. Next, negotiate in advance with other firms for access to their buildings, networks, and hardware to run the company's existing IT operations or to continue manufacturing and shipping products. In the case of IT, there are companies that will perform mirror operations of existing IT applications, so that if a data center is out of commission, a company can switch immediately to another. Meanwhile, business partners or suppliers can make products and provide services.

Because of the durability of the Internet, making sure that internal access is up and running is crucial in today's business and government environments. Typical strategies include use of internal private network providers, often several simultaneously, in case one goes down; dispersing work across many physical locations; beefing up access security so that people can't log on to applications they are not authorized to perform; physically protecting servers and other telecommunications equipment in more secure locations.

To pull all these elements together, companies can rely on the Internet, as the response to 9-11 demonstrated. While cell phones, regular telephone communications, and other networks crashed or had so much traffic that they choked, the Internet kept on functioning. The reason is that the U.S. military designed the original Internet so that it could withstand nuclear war. It was decentralized so that computers all over the country (now all over the world) could dynamically reroute messages without needing anyone to instruct them to do so. That strategy of decentralization made it possible for the Internet to operate seamlessly. People were able to check on each other quickly after 9-11, using the Internet. IBM workers, for example, used Sametime communications over the Internet to check on all their colleagues and employees throughout the New York area and in Washington, D.C., accounting for thousands of people within hours. In New York before 9-11, many cell phone calls had been routed through equipment located high on the now nonexistent World Trade Towers. On that date, many became useless by mid morning.

What is required is clear: Communications must remain up and running to ensure the operation and protection of organizations and people. Relying on multiple types of equipment, processes, and locations is essential. As we increasingly become an economy operating in the Information Age, these kinds of considerations must make the short list of the few, the vital, the essential "must do's."

Physical security of buildings and people represents the other great challenge of the new normalcy. Major companies have been working on the problem for years, using surveillance cameras outside of buildings, putting up cement barriers at entrances to block potential car bombs, keeping people out who had no business in a building, escorting visitors to their destinations, tracking and profiling potentially dangerous people (airlines have done this for years), and inspecting bags and packages. There will be more of such actions as developers of various technologies create new ways of maintaining security. In the new normalcy, people and enterprises must work together more closely and consciously on the security of information, facilities, and people.

The factor of dispersal as a source of strength and a means of protection is relevant to the strength and security of the United States as a nation. Geography has helped considerably. America is protected by mighty moats—oceans on both sides—and is spread east to west across the North American continent. It is too dispersed, too varied, too many-sided to be vulnerable to single attacks. The truth is that one could wipe out New York and Los Angeles, and while it would stagger the economy, business would continue. The country would go on, however crippled. This is a big country, spread out with redundant resources all over the place. We have many cities that do what is done in New York and Los Angeles. Farmers in Virginia can raise corn, just as others do in Nebraska. Automobiles are made not only in Detroit, but also in Tennessee and Ohio. Our military bases cover the country. Our highway and air traffic control networks blanket the continent. There are multiple copies of everything we can do scattered across the country. Since there is so much of everything, knocking out one or more capabilities, places, or locations can hardly bring the nation to its knees. As tragic as it is, for example, when the vice presidents of a stock brokerage firm are killed in the Twin Towers, there are thousands of other vice presidents scattered across the country with parallel levels of education, expertise, and experience who can lead a stock brokerage operation after a 9-11 catastrophe. Maintaining organizational and operational diversity in a healthy economy across such a large nation is itself a form of protection against attack and a source of security.

There are national strategies that also need to be implemented, some already suggested in earlier chapters, others warranting attention here. They are a combination of personal and national initiatives. On the one hand, there are things that must be done at a national level—such as conducting the war on terrorism—but there are other actions to be performed individually. In combination, the two can make the new normalcy a sustainable way of life that is both safe and prosperous. So what strategies should be deployed? We believe there are several that need to be implemented simultaneously, in a holistic fashion. They build on prior experience and thus leverage what already has worked.

On a national basis, rooting out those who would attack the nation, kill its people, and destroy its assets is, of course, an immediate requirement. While this is the path which the Bush administration is already following, the campaign against terrorism must be unrelenting. We cannot afford to let our guard down or be lulled into complacency when our enemies lie dormant—until their next attack. National resolve demands that we use our assets and know-how to protect ourselves with a proactive strategy, one that seeks out the enemy and thwarts its plans.

A go-it-alone strategy does not make sense. Our post-9-11 coalition building demonstrates the need to meet the global threat of terrorism with a global response. Anything less endangers the entire effort and compromises the chances for success. As great as our assets and know-how are, we cannot alone defeat the worldwide threat of terrorism and its many sponsors. Technology alone is not enough. It cannot replace intelligence on the ground, which depends on international allies. The al-Qaeda alone has trained an estimated 70,000 to 80,000 people now scattered all over the world. And it is only one terrorist group! Only by eradicating multiple terrorist groups will we put terrorists on the defensive.

The world faces terrorism as a constant in international affairs, liable to emerge anywhere, anytime. While terrorist acts declined in Northern Ireland and in Spain's Basque country, for example, terrorists attacked the Indian Parliament in December 2001, creating an Indian-Pakistani crisis. In the Middle East, the abiding Palestinian-Israeli conflict has kept the Middle East in turmoil, with the constant threat of spreading. A crackdown on suicide bombers alienates the more extremist Palestinians, the Hamas, which portends increased problems in the Middle East in a cycle of violence and instability that involves the United States and its Middle Eastern allies.

For the United States, as the world's most powerful nation, there is no escaping the fallout and repercussions of terrorism. Such has been the case with America's decades-long involvement with the Palestinian-Israeli conflict. Our reading of modern Arabic history suggests it will not be resolved soon in a peaceful way, following ups and downs. Meanwhile, American support for Israel faces a transformation as other priorities come to the fore and the Arab states exhibit political tensions within their own borders. Americans are becoming more sympathetic to Israel's claims that Palestinians are not nationalists, but rather terrorists. Saudi Arabia, long seen as an American ally, is increasingly being viewed as a hotbed of economic and political support for Arab terrorists. Iraq remains America's number one rogue country, targeted for attack if the U.S. could be assured that other Arab states would not get in the way. The replacement of the pre-9-11 government in Afghanistan with a new coalition government is already sending signals to other countries that the U.S. is willing to attempt real nation building, despite an historic reluctance to play that role. Overall, the U.S. must remain tuned to the twists and turns of political events around the world, not just in the Middle East, and must respond appropriately in fighting terrorism.

Taking a medium- to long-term view, the concept of homeland defense implemented by the Bush administration may turn out to be the most significant by-product of 9-11. Despite the concern of many Americans about the potential for compromising civil liberties, coordinated homeland defense can help to preserve our civil liberties, while improving our defense and security. That would result from the coordinated search for terrorists, in combining the talents and assets of the CIA, FBI, NSA, IRS, state police, and local law enforcement officials. By leveraging computer technology and sharing information, good old-fashioned police work can be done within our boundaries for civil liberties. The opportunity exists to improve security by drawing on the efficiencies involved in greater coordination.

Respect and support for the Constitution and the values of the founding fathers remain too strongly embedded in our culture to be brushed aside. The balance of power provided by the separation of powers—executive, legislative, judicial—can be expected to provide protection against extremes as it normally has in the past. State constitutions have a similar balance of power, as part of the legal backdrop against which to implement more closely coordinated security matters. Critics can correctly point out breaches in civil liberties: Japanese Americans interned during World War II, profiling of Arab Americans questioned today by the

FBI. But take the emotion out of such examples and we can make two observations: The numbers involved are so small that they must be regarded as exceptions to an otherwise larger pattern of respecting civil liberties, and the American public historically has been willing to tolerate some flexibility in the preservation of civil liberties. Civil liberties have never been absolutes. In practice, they are malleable enough so that the government can apply sufficient flexibility in responding to specific threats to the overall welfare of the nation. In the long run, at least, justice normally prevailed.

Against the fear of "Big Brother" compromising civil liberties, there is the prospect of greater protection which will come from more efficient operations in our security apparatus. Before 9-11, major intelligence and law enforcement agencies operated in relative isolation from each other, the direct result of explicit legislation defining their missions narrowly and differently from each other. We can change the laws so that they have to work more closely together, share more information, and use each other's equipment and other assets. Tentative steps in this direction took place when the U.S. Congress passed enabling legislation in October, 2001 to begin the process.

Over time, we can expect that the cost of technology for these agencies will decline as they share more data. Redundancies of staffs and agencies will be reduced, just as occurs when two companies merge and improve their overall efficiencies. As a lesson from business, such mergers and better coordination will improve the timely availability of higher quality information with which to block terrorists and round them up. Typically, discussions about benefits of the Information Age have focused on business. Now we can expect to see them applied to homeland defense.

With history as an indicator, homeland defense will focus first on physical security of North America, applying current laws, governmental practices, technologies, and the economic wherewithal of the nation. The record of performance has been good; only once in the nineteenth century did the government fail in a major way—in the War of 1812, when it was unable to prevent the British from invading the United States and seizing the capital of Washington, D.C. In the twentieth century, there were four breakdowns in security—in 1912, when a few Mexicans invaded the United States, leading to General John Pershing's pursuit of them deep into Mexico; on December 7, 1941 when Japan bombed Pearl Harbor; and during World War II, when there was a small Japanese invasion of a remote island off Alaska. Both, however, were minor events. Then there was 9-11.

In terms of security, the United States has always used a wide-angle lens, focusing on all of North America. In the world of the new normalcy, we can expect that Canada and the U.S. will continue their coordination in security matters. That will happen because it is of mutual interest. The new element will be Mexico, where the outlook is promising. There is mounting evidence that the Fox administration in Mexico sees itself as part of a larger North American economic and social sphere of great benefit to individual Mexicans. NAFTA preconditioned both nations to cooperate economically, while the rapid influx of Mexicans into the U.S. in the last third of the twentieth century created a large Hispanic, mutually supportive culture, in sync with that of the United States.

Viewed together, all these elements—values, population makeup, national and homeland defense policies, and economic realities—have the making of an effective program to root out terrorism. The current initiative also borrows tactics from the experiences of the liberal democratic societies of Western Europe, which have a half-century of experience in dealing with terrorism. At the practical level, for instance, the British know how to minimize Irish car bombs, the Spanish how to hunt down Basque terrorists, and the Israelis in the Middle East how to gather intelligence and pinpoint retaliation.

Recent history presents a harsh comparison. Entire cities are not being blown up, as happened to the British, Germans, and Japanese during World War II. Tens of thousands of people are not being killed every month, as happened during the Iran-Iraq wars of the 1980s. Fewer people are killed in the United States by terrorists than die from automobile accidents or are injured on the job. Nonetheless, any deaths from terrorism are unacceptable and could escalate to catastrophic levels. For us as individual Americans, we have essentially three things to do:

First, as public officials urge, Americans should be cautious and scrupulous in making sure there is no strange, possibly dangerous situation around them. Neighborhood watch programs for decades have shown the way; now their watchdog practices need to be applied in public spaces and at work. What is unusual should be suspected, inspected, and questioned. We must make sure that common-sense security procedures exist in our place of work. When something doesn't look right, we must alert public officials so they can deal with the situation.

Second, we must support the government's elimination of threats to the nation anywhere in the world. Our national leadership relies on public backing expressed through opinion surveys, demonstrated by congressional action, and supported by individual actions, from enlisting in the armed services to volunteering to join in community-based security programs.

As part of their sense of involvement, Americans need to pay more attention to international affairs, learn more about political science, and become more aware of American history. Compared with other advanced nations, Americans tend to neglect these three areas that are part of responsible citizenship. In our schools, more American and world history should be taught at all levels through college years. Those of us out of school need to read more about these areas and watch public affairs programs on the networks and cable, particularly on PBS and C-SPAN. Understanding the context of our lives is part of responsible participation and citizenship. America does not live in isolation from the rest of the world, as 9-11 reminded us. The U.S. demonstrated the same global closeness when its planes commuted to Afghanistan from Missouri on bombing missions in the fall of 2001. Effectively, Afghanistan became as close as Canada. It's as though the Middle East were across the border where Canada is situated. If Canada were a threat, would we not want to know a great deal more about the Canadians and their internal affairs? Of course, and the same logic applies to the larger world.

Third, we must be vigilant about compromising freedom of action and civil liberties. The temptation to trade them away in exchange for physical security is great. That temptation—which is what it is—has always been presented to Americans during a national crisis. Some Americans bought into it but fortunately most did not. In the end, civil liberties and personal freedom of movement, expression, and thought survived. The key point is that Americans can have personal security without surrendering personal freedoms. It is the genius of the American system. It is simply now our turn to demonstrate its durability.

AN AGE OF DECENCY?

A sense of shared vulnerability after 9-11, followed immediately by the steps taken to provide security, pointed the country toward an age of decency, one marked by civility and a greater sense of shared community and of caring for one another. An introspective mood spread across the nation, nowhere more obvious than in its religious practices. Americans did what they have always done in times of national crisis, they went to church.

This is the characteristic way in which Americans build the nation's resolve whenever we face a problem of historic proportions. We turn to our values, our faiths, and to our heritage of inspirational songs and prayers, all of which have sustained us in prior wars, during depressions, and through natural catastrophes. Religion girds us for action and commitment to a righteous cause. Going to church has always been one sure signal that Americans were beginning to put aside their differences and were starting the process of joint commitment.

This ritual is important to recognize because no national strategy will have enough power to deal with the new normalcy without a powerful level of resolve. This represents the major message in this book: confronting the new normalcy calls for resolve that is open-ended, ready to go where nobody yet knows, and aiming for a conclusion that will not necessarily be marked by a specific event, such as a peace treaty or formal surrender. In sum, the new normalcy demands a resolve different from what we have known in the past.

Sustaining such an open-ended initiative requires a high level of confidence that the end result will be a good one and a sense of purpose that is unwavering. This is more than taking revenge for terrorism in a cold-blooded manner. It is about an abiding commitment to eradicate a problem, to focus on objectives, and to apply whatever technologies, assets, intelligence, and experience we have as Americans.

In the weeks following 9-11, religion once again fortified American spirit and determination. Attendance at church services rose by some 10 percent all over the nation. National memorial services and emotion-filled funerals in churches of different faiths demonstrated the role of formal religion. When the press began reporting that church attendance was dropping back to pre-9-11 levels, it missed the point about the religious involvement of Americans. An increase in church attendance has been slow but steady since the 1990s, as the population grew older and the nation became more reflective. We cannot measure religious influence only in terms of participation in religious services. Major studies of religious involvement in the United States conclude that Americans overall are some of the most committed to religion in the world. Besides steeling people with resolve, religion encourages a gentler, more caring attitude. It puts the mundane in perspective and pro-vides a context within which to search for purpose in life.

AN AMERICAN TIME, SOME FINAL THOUGHTS

Two historians who have looked at long-term patterns in American life have amassed an impressive body of evidence that provides a long view of what we face. William Strauss and Neil Howe have identified common experiences of generations of Americans and have concluded that we can speak about specific generations sharing characteristic values and experiences. This is more than knowing where they were on December 7 or on the day that President Kennedy was shot. The two historians have identified profound, fundamentally influential cycles of behavior that repeat themselves—four basic styles or rhythms of life, which they call *turnings*. Briefly summarized, they are: (1) a "high," such as the U.S. experience between the end of World War II and the early 1960s; (2) an "awakening," a period in which there is a revolution in consciousness, such as we experienced between the time of President Kennedy's assassination to the end of the 1970s; (3) an "unraveling," an era of self-indulgence, such as we had in the 1920s and again in the 1980s and 1990s; and (4) a period of crisis, normally a time of war or the Great Depression of the 1930s. Each turning has profoundly affected the generation coming of age. Strauss and Howe believe, as do we, that America is now entering another fourth turning. In that phase of the nation's life, its mood and behavior are characterized by a renewed sense of community and commitment, such as patriotism and a resolve to win a war. In our time, it is the war on terrorism.

Those who lived during the protest era of the Vietnam War are discovering what older generations already knew, that the current wave of patriotism is a very positive, reassuring force. Renewed patriotism and a strong sense of what it means to be an American have triggered fresh interest in American values and history, as well as pride in our political institutions and freedoms. In how many countries could someone like Brian Lamb direct a TV station like C-SPAN, in which every kind of political process and event is presented to the public unedited, unvarnished, "from gavel to gavel"? Meanwhile, Americans have shown themselves as a gentler, kinder people. Their monetary contributions to various funds to help the families who lost members in New York and Washington, D.C. ran over a billion dollars in less than 45 days, evidence of the solicitous hands of individual Americans reaching out.

When *Time* magazine and CNN conducted a poll of the nation's mood in the fall of 2001, a gratifying and encouraging image of Americans emerged. People reported that family reunions had become more important, rifts with relatives were in decline, divorce lawyers even saw a drop in business. The American Bible Society reported that fall 2001 sales of the quintessential American book, the Holy Bible, were up 42 percent over the previous fall. Sales of the Koran shot up, as well, as Americans turned to that holy book for insights into the minds of the terrorists. In short, the new normalcy brought forth a renewal of traditional values and, for good measure, showed a desire to learn about others, a harbinger of national empathy.

September 11 also ushered in a time to honor heroes and follow leaders. Historically, American individualism has always made it easier to find them when needed. They emerged without fanfare as a plain and simple matter of doing their jobs and of defending others and themselves—New York firefighters, emergency medical teams, police officers, all rushing to the Twin Towers of the World Trade Center, military personnel rushing to the destroyed portion of the Pentagon to rescue colleagues, passengers and crew fighting terrorists on an airplane over Pennsylvania. They were not told what to do. They knew what they had to do.

Before 9-11, President Bush was given very low marks for leadership qualities. After 9-11, most Americans praised the high quality of his leadership. Mayor Giuliani went from being a mayor with marital problems to being the most popular politician in New York's history, lionized by the entire nation, named Person of the Year by *Time* magazine, hailed as "mayor of the nation." Bush and Giuliani earned their accolades as leaders, as did firefighters and police officers earn their honors as heros. For the new normalcy, new leaders and new heroes provide inspiration, as well as answers. They represent Americans as individuals facing up to their responsibilities to act, to lead, to demonstrate American values in action. They stand out among the reasons why Americans as individuals and the United States as a nation can make this a safer world for all of us.

Let the wife of the second president of the United States, Abigail Adams, have the final word. Writing in 1778 in the darkest days of the American Revolution, when no sane, practical person would have bet that the colonists could ever defeat the most powerful army of the Western world, she argued, "If we do not lay out ourselves in the service of mankind, whom should we serve?" She was thoroughly American in her outlook before the United States even existed!

INDEX

The *Financial Times* delivers a world of business news.

Use the Risk-Free Trial Voucher below!

To stay ahead in today's business world you need to be well-informed on a daily basis. And not just on the national level. You need a news source that closely monitors the entire world of business, and then delivers it in a concise, quick-read format.

With the *Financial Times* you get the major stories from every region of the world. Reports found nowhere else. You get business, management, politics, economics, technology and more.

Now you can try the *Financial Times* for 4 weeks, absolutely risk free. And better yet, if you wish to continue receiving the *Financial Times* you'll get great savings off the regular subscription rate. Just use the voucher below.

8 reasons why you should read the Financial Times for 4 weeks RISK-FREE!

To help you stay current with significant
developments in the world economy ...
and to assist you to make informed business
decisions — the Financial Times brings you:

❶ Fast, meaningful overviews of international affairs ... plus daily
briefings on major world news.

❷ Perceptive coverage of economic, business, financial and political
developments with special focus on emerging markets.

❸ More international business news than any other publication.

❹ Sophisticated financial analysis and commentary on world market
activity plus stock quotes from over 30 countries.

❺ Reports on international companies and a section on global investing.

❻ Specialized pages on management, marketing, advertising and
technological innovations from all parts of the world.

❼ Highly valued single-topic special reports (over 200 annually)
on countries, industries, investment opportunities, technology and more.

❽ The Saturday Weekend FT section — a globetrotter's guide to
leisure-time activities around the world: the arts, fine dining, travel,
sports and more.

For Special Offer See Over

FT FINANCIAL TIMES
World business newspaper